An Independent and Accountable IMF

Geneva Reports on the World Economy 1

International Center for Monetary and Banking Studies

11 A Avenue de la Paix
1202 Geneva
Switzerland

Tel: +41 22 734 9548
Fax: +41 22 733 3853

Centre for Economic Policy Research

90–98 Goswell Road
London EC1V 7RR
UK

Tel: +44 (0)171 878 2900
Fax: +44 (0)171 878 2999
Email: cepr@cepr.org
Website: www.cepr.org

British Library Cataloguing in Publication Data
A catalogue record for this book is available from the British Library

ISBN: 1 898128 45 6

Printed and bound in the UK by Information Press, Oxford

An Independent and Accountable IMF

Geneva Reports on the World Economy 1

José De Gregorio
Universidad de Chile, Santiago

Barry Eichengreen
University of California at Berkeley, CEPR and NBER

Takatoshi Ito
Hitotsubashi University, Tokyo, TCER and NBER

Charles Wyplosz
Graduate Institute of International Studies, Geneva, and CEPR

ICMB INTERNATIONAL CENTER
FOR MONETARY
AND BANKING STUDIES

CIMB CENTRE INTERNATIONAL
D'ETUDES MONETAIRES
ET BANCAIRES

International Center for Monetary and Banking Studies (ICMB)

The International Center for Monetary and Banking Studies was created in 1973 as an independent, non-profit foundation. It is associated with Geneva's Graduate Institute of International Studies. The Center sponsors international conferences, public lectures, original research and publications. It has earned a solid reputation in the Swiss and international banking community where it is known for its contribution to bridging the gap between theory and practice in the field of international banking and finance.

Centre for Economic Policy Research (CEPR)

The Centre for Economic Policy Research is a network of over 450 Research Fellows, based primarily in European universities. The Centre coordinates its Fellows' research activities and communicates their results to the public and private sectors. CEPR is an entrepreneur, developing research initiatives with the producers, consumers and sponsors of research. Established in 1983, CEPR is a European economics research organization with uniquely wide-ranging scope and activities.

CEPR is a registered educational charity. Institutional (core) finance for the Centre is provided by major grants from the Economic and Social Research Council, under which an ESRC Resource Centre operates within CEPR; the Esmée Fairbairn Charitable Trust and the Bank of England. The Centre is also supported by the European Central Bank; the Bank for International Settlements; 22 national central banks and 45 companies. None of these organizations gives prior review to the Centre's publications, nor do they necessarily endorse the views expressed therein.

The Centre is pluralist and non-partisan, bringing economic research to bear on the analysis of medium- and long-run policy questions. CEPR research may include views on policy, but the Executive Committee of the Centre does not give prior review to its publications, and the Centre takes no institutional policy positions. The opinions expressed in this report are those of the authors and not those of the Centre for Economic Policy Research

About the Authors

José De Gregorio is Professor of Economics at the University of Chile. He has served as Director of Economic Policy at the Chilean Finance Ministry and on the staff of the IMF. He has written numerous and influential analyses on international economics, including capital account management and exchange rates in the Chilean economy.

Barry Eichengreen is John L. Simpson Professor of Economics and Political Science at the University of California, Berkeley. He has written widely on the international monetary system, past, present and future. In 1997–8 he was Senior Policy Advisor at the IMF, where he worked on hedge funds and the Asian crisis, capital account liberalization and proposals for strengthening the international financial architecture.

Takatoshi Ito is Professor of Economics at Hitotsubashi University and Research Associate of NBER. He was for two years Senior Economist at the IMF, at the time of the Mexican crisis. He was responsible for the preparation of the Fund's reports on *International Capital Markets, 1995* and *1996*. He is an advisor to the Finance Minister of Thailand, and has led missions of various Japanese organizations to other crisis countries in Asia, 1997–9.

Charles Wyplosz is Professor of International Economics at the Graduate Institute of International Studies in Geneva and Director of the International Macreconomics Programme of CEPR. He is a frequent consultant to the IMF, the World Bank, the European Commission and has advised the government of the Russian Federation. He has made a number of contributions to the European Monetary Union and is a specialist on currency crises. He is Director of the International Center for Monetary and Banking Studies.

Contents

List of Conference Participants

Krister Andersson   Chief Economist, SE Banken, Stockholm – Sweden.

Urban Bäckström   President and Chairman, Sveriges Riksbank, Stockholm – Sweden.

Jeanne Barras-Zwahlen   Senior Economist, Credit Suisse Private Banking, Geneva – Switzerland.

Jean-Pierre Beguelin   Chief Economist, Pictet & Cie, Geneva – Switzerland.

Benoît Coeuré   Conseiller Economique, Direction du Trésor, Ministère des Finances, Paris – France.

Giovanni A. Colombo   International Monetary and Financial Affairs, Swiss Federal Department of Finance, Bern – Switzerland.

Andrew Crockett   General Manager, Bank for International Settlements, Basel – Switzerland.

Jon Cunliffe   Deputy Director, International Finance Division, HM Treasury, London – United Kingdom.

Jean-Pierre Danthine   Professor and Director of FAME programme, DEEP, Université de Lausanne, Lausanne – Switzerland and CEPR.

Pierre Darier   Managing Partner, Darier, Hentsch & Cie, Geneva – Switzerland.

José De Gregorio   Professor of Economics at the University of Chile – Chile.

Jacques Delpla   Senior European Economist, Barclays Capital, Paris – France.

Bengt Dennis   Advisor, SE Banken, Stockholm – Sweden.

Cédric Dupont	Assistant Professor, Political Science Department, Graduate Institute of International Studies, Geneva – Switzerland.
Barry Eichengreen	Professor of Economics and Political Science, University of California, Berkeley – USA and CEPR.
Hans Genberg	Professor of Economics/Director, International Center for Monetary and Banking Studies, Geneva – Switzerland.
Giorgio Gomel	Head of the International Division, Research Department, Banca d'Italia, Rome – Italy.
Pablo Guidotti	Secretario de Hacienda, Ministerio de Economia, Buenos Aires – Argentina.
Werner Hermann	Deputy Director, International Monetary Relations, Swiss National Bank, Zurich – Switzerland.
Philipp Hildebrand	Senior Managing Director, Moore Capital Strategy Group, London – United Kingdom.
Paul Inderbinden	Economist, IMF and International Financial Affairs, Swiss Federal Department of Finance, Bern – Switzerland.
Takatoshi Ito	Professor of Economics, Hitotsubashi University – Japan.
Nicolas Krul	Financial Adviser, London – United Kingdom.
Jean-Pierre Landau	Managing Director, French Banking Association, Former Executive Director for France at IMF, Paris – France.
Flemming Larsen	Deputy Director, Research Department, International Monetary Fund, USA.
Ian MacFarlane	Governor of the Reserve Bank of Australia, Sydney – Australia.
Giuseppe Maresca	Head, Division of International Financial Institutions, Department of the Treasury – Italy.
Michel Mordasini	Head of Section, Multilateral Financial Institutions, Swiss Federal Office for Foreign Economic Affairs, Bern – Switzerland.

Thomas Moser	Economic Adviser, International Monetary Relations, Swiss National Bank, Zurich – Switzerland.
Shijuro Ogata	Former Deputy Governor for International Relations, Bank of Japan, Tokyo – Japan.
Yung Chul Park	Professor/Chairman of the Board Directors, Department of Economics, Korea University/Korea Exchange Bank, Seoul – Korea.
Guillermo Perry	Chief Economist, Latin America Region, The World Bank – USA
Richard Portes	President, Centre for Economic Policy Research, London – United Kingdom.
Klaus Regling	Managing Director, Moore Capital Strategy Group, London – United Kingdom.
Jean-Pierre Roth	Vice-Chairman of the Governing Board, Swiss National Bank, Bern – Switzerland.
Hans-Jörg Rudloff	Chairman of the Executive Committee, Barclays Capital, London – United Kingdom.
Claudio Segré	Banker and Chairman, Argus Fund, Geneva – Switzerland.
Ms Louellen Stedman	Deputy Director, International Monetary Policy Office, Department of the Treasury, Washington – USA.
Alexander Swoboda	Senior Policy Advisor & Resident Scholar, International Monetary Fund, Washington – USA.
Peter Tschopp	Director, Graduate Institute of International Studies, Geneva – Switzerland.
Charles Wyplosz	Professor of International Economics, Graduate Institute of International Studies, Geneva – Switzerland and CEPR.
Jean Zwahlen	Vice-President, Union Bancaire Privée, Geneva – Switzerland.

List of Tables

List of Figures

List of Boxes

Acknowledgements

This Report was presented at a conference on 'The IMF After Mexico' held on 7 May 1999 in Geneva. The conference was organized by the Center for International Monetary and Banking Studies, Geneva and CEPR. The authors thank Cédric Dupont, Richard Portes and conference participants for comments and suggestions, Xavier Debrun for superb research assistance, Romesh Vaitilingam for editing, Nicolas Guigas and Marcel Peter for recording the discussion, Valérie Laxton, Birgit Dam, Tessa Ogden and Kate Millward for their hard and effective work in organizing this event. Barry Eichengreen thanks the Ford Foundation for support through the Berkeley Project on New International Financial Architecture. The work represents the authors' views and does not necessarily represent the views of their affiliated institutions, past, present or future.

Foreword

Current financial crises appear to differ fundamentally from others since the 1930s: they occur with more violence, they are harder to foresee and they leave deeper scars. Perhaps most significantly, foreign exchange and debt crises often occur simultaneously with banking crises, and they now tend to hit the emerging market countries.

The new world economy needs an International Monetary Fund which recognizes how these problems have changed. The Fund's response to date has been to mobilize ever larger rescue packages and to go deeper into domestic structural conditions, and yet it has often failed to achieve its stated aims. The Fund's traditional views of exchange rate regimes and the desirability of unfettered capital mobility no longer correspond to the situation of many developing countries. The main shareholders are from the developed countries. Does this mean that the IMF must radically transform itself in the future or even, as has been suggested, that it has become useless?

The first joint effort between CEPR and ICMB was the volume *Threats to International Financial Stability* (Cambridge University Press, 1987), which made a mark on the discussion of what was then the 'debt crisis'. Despite the changing circumstances, its analyses are still relevant as background for the current discussion. As the role of the IMF has moved into centre stage of the debate on 'international financial architecture', we thought it highly appropriate to renew our joint efforts with work on the future of the IMF.

These issues were discussed in depth at our conference on 'The IMF After Mexico', based on a first draft of this Report. Sessions focused on the way in which the IMF has dealt with the new crises; who should pay for the crises; how the IMF could be reformed to handle future crises better; and whether the IMF is actually in need of major reform. The title of the Report reflects its emphasis not only on the Fund's policies and procedures, but also on its mandate.[1] The conference was attended by many of the key figures in the field, with a wide range of collective experience in handling financial crises. We believe that the resulting discussion and proposals will be of great interest to both researchers and decision-makers.

The conference took place on 7 May 1999 in Geneva and was organized by the International Center for Monetary and Banking Studies (ICMB) and CEPR. We would especially like to thank Valérie Laxton, Tessa Ogden and Kate Millward for their hard and effective work in organizing this event. We are also grateful to Romesh Vaitilingam for providing invaluable comments, suggestions and revisions throughout the writing process. The usefulness of this Report is partly a function of the speed with which it has been produced. For that we thank Linda Machin, Sue Chapman and her colleagues.

On this occasion, we extend our special thanks to Charles Wyplosz, without whose initiative and enthusiasm this renewal of our collaboration would not have been possible.

Richard Portes   Jean-Pierre Roth
CEPR   ICMB

19 May 1999

---

1. For an analogous focus, see the CEPR Report, *Independent and Accountable: A New Mandate for the Bank of England* (CEPR, 1993).

Executive Summary

This Report, the first Geneva Report on the World Economy (organized by the Center for International Monetary and Banking Studies, Geneva, in conjunction with the Centre for Economic Policy Research), analyses the increasingly severe financial crises in emerging markets that have punctuated the final years of the twentieth century. The Report focuses on the role of the International Monetary Fund (IMF) in predicting, averting and managing the volatility associated with open, liquid and internationally integrated financial markets.

Sometimes referred to as 'high-tech financial crises' or 'the first financial crises of the twenty-first century', these episodes of turbulence have become more violent, disruptive and difficult to predict and manage because they are now centred in the capital account of developing countries' balance of payments. This contrasts with earlier crises, which were rooted in imbalances in the current account, but the IMF has yet to integrate this evolution into its diagnoses, procedures and conditions.

To date, the Fund's response to crisis has been to rely on larger and more heavily front-loaded loans, disbursed more rapidly and accompanied by conditionality that mixes old-fashioned macroeconomic adjustment with deep structural interventions. Whether this approach is appropriate to today's new circumstances remains open to question. Also at issue, is whether the Fund has succeeded in adapting its staff and governance structure in a way that allows it to cope with these new challenges.

The new IMF emphasis on data dissemination and transparency is welcome. But the belief that this will strengthen market discipline sufficiently to head off crises before they start is naive. There are also good reasons to doubt that the Fund's aspiration to identify reliable early warning signals of impending crises is likely to succeed.

The Fund must rethink both its traditional recommendation that crisis countries impose tough monetary and fiscal policies and its recent tendency to provide ever-larger balance of payments financing. Restarting an economy that is the victim of a severe credit crunch may require a wholly different approach, including the restructuring of foreign currency debts – both public and private – and the adoption of reflationary measures.

There is a strong economic case for the IMF to continue to play a major international role. Yet its governance structure and the representation of its member countries are anachronistic and must be reformed.

In particular, the role of the Executive Board is unsatisfactory. Directors are often overwhelmed by the IMF staff and its considerable agenda-setting power. What is more, their decision-making is driven by national agendas, specifically those of the principal shareholders.

To rectify these problems, we make the following proposals:

■ The IMF should be made truly independent and accountable. Insulating the Executive Board from the politically driven agendas of national governments would permit it to focus more efficiently on surveillance and conditionality. This requires amending the Articles of Agreement on which the Fund is founded.

■ But independence would be counterproductive without adequate accountability and transparency. The Interim Committee is the logical body to provide oversight of the Fund and hold the Executive Directors accountable for their decisions. If it were given the power to remove Directors who pursue private agendas, the Interim Committee could fulfil these roles. In this way, the power not only of the Board but also of the Interim Committee would be strengthened while at the same time creating a clear separation of roles and responsibilities.

■ The Board should be accountable not only to governments but also to the public at large. Publishing detailed minutes of Board meetings, requiring decisions through voting rather than consensus, and publishing voting records of the Executive Directors would move the Fund into the modern era of transparency.

■ The perception of excessive influence from the US Treasury –
unavoidable given its geographical and intellectual proximity
to the Fund – would be lessened by reducing from 85% to 80%
of votes the current 'supermajority' needed for the most
important IMF decisions. This change would mean that no one
country had a veto.

1 The International Financial Institutions: New Roles in a New World

This first chapter examines the role of capital mobility and the IMF's response to the emergence of active financial markets in developing countries. It takes stock of the rapidly accumulating evidence on currency and banking crises and on contagion. It observes the widening of the list of 'fundamentals' that trigger crises. It explores how the IMF has responded with faster programmes and larger loans, and with a form of conditionality that combines structural reforms with classic macroeconomic measures. And it asks whether the IMF is adjusting its staff and governance structure so that it is better positioned to cope with these new challenges.

1.1 Twenty-first century crises

The Mexican crisis of 1994–5 was a shock not just to financial markets but to the IMF itself. The peso's 15% devaluation on 20 December 1994 quickly turned into a rout, as huge private capital outflows precipitated a 50% depreciation of the currency within a week. When Mexico and the IMF began negotiating a support package, it quickly became clear that unprecedented amounts of assistance would be required. Capital outflows were swamping Mexico's quota with the Fund, not to mention the resources of the IMF itself.

Shell-shocked IMF officials were face to face with the first financial crisis of the twenty-first century. In the words of the Managing Director:

Mexico's crisis has been described as the first financial crisis of the twenty-first century, meaning the first major financial crisis to hit an emerging market economy in the new world of globalized financial markets. And this says a lot about its significance. The increasing

1

international integration of financial markets in the past 10–15 years has brought great benefits, by fostering a more efficient allocation of global savings and boosting investment and growth in many countries. But there is a downside: vastly increased financial flows across national borders have also made countries that participate in international financial markets more vulnerable to adverse shifts in market sentiment: such shifts, though generally related to concerns about economic fundamentals and policy shortcomings, can often be delayed, sudden, massive and destabilizing. Furthermore, financial globalization has increased the speed with which disturbances in one country can be transmitted to others. So financial globalization, though both a product of and a contributor to the economic progress of our time, has heightened the challenges of preventing and resolving financial crises.

And it is no accident that this crisis hit one of the most successful developing economies. An essential ingredient in the success of Mexico in the past decade – as with all other successful developing economies – has been its increased openness to the world economy and integration into international financial markets.   Camdessus (1995)

IMF Managing Director Michel Camdessus was discovering the unintended consequences of the capital mobility that his institution had been advocating for nearly ten years. But what exactly was he lamenting? The loss of control of the exchange rate? The cost of the IMF-led loan? The impotence of textbook stabilization measures? The severity of the recession that followed? The need for new forms of IMF conditionality?

Camdessus was unquestionably right that a major change was underway. But neither he nor anyone else fully anticipated the extent of the difficulties that the IMF would confront and the severity of the criticism soon to be directed at the institution. Within a few years, there would be many more 'twenty-first century crises': Asia, Russia and Brazil among others, all absorbing huge financial resources yet displaying an alarming resistance to the traditional IMF medicine.

What was different about this new world?

■   First, private capital flows were strikingly large relative to GDP. Current account deficits of 8% could persist because of the financing provided by private capital flows. But when those flows changed direction, the shock to countries dependent on foreign financing was now unprecedentedly large. In other words, the capital account now swamped the current account. Exchange rates and interest rates now responded to capital flows, no longer to changes in the balance between merchandise imports and merchandise exports.

■ Second, the decline in transactions costs and the development of high-tech financial products allowed capital flows to reverse in an instant. Derivative products traded 'over the counter' allowed investors to leverage their bets – to take huge positions without putting up much money of their own. Foreign currency reserves, no matter how large, were dwarfed by the liquidity of the markets. In the Mexican case, capital outflows were so large and rapid that much of the damage to the peso was already done long before the IMF arrived on the scene.

■ Third, the relationship between crises and macroeconomic fundamentals had loosened. The initial devaluation of the peso was not inconsistent with observers' *ex ante* assessments, but the magnitude of the ensuing collapse was wholly unexpected. After all, Mexico had just joined NAFTA, a move that recognized its macroeconomic and structural progress over the previous *sixenio*. And not only did markets seem to be over-reacting, but they also continued to attack a currency that had already fallen to a level thought to be more than reasonable. The IMF, as fire-fighter, could not contain the blaze. Its ability to control the system set up at Bretton Woods exactly 50 years previously was cast into doubt, a most unwelcome way to celebrate the anniversary.

Box 1.1 **The first crisis of the twenty-first century? Chile in 1982**

Mexico's crisis happened in the absence of any serious fiscal imbal-ance. Private spending had been driving the country's current account deficit and it was not thought that a private current account deficit could be a serious problem. The Latin American debt crises of the 1980s had been associated with large fiscal imbalances, with the notable exception of Chile's. Like Mexico in 1994 or some Asian countries in 1997, Chile's fiscal position was strong in the early 1980s (see Table B1.1). Yet its current account deficit rose to 14% in 1981, and rather than financing investment, the deficit was associated with an increase in consumption and a construction boom. Both were the consequence of financial liberalization and the fixing of the exchange rate from June 1979 to June 1982.

The real exchange rate appreciated significantly over this period and was clearly misaligned by 1981. The eventual correction was sharp and

continued

Box 1.1 continued

the ensuing depreciation was similar in magnitude to those seen more recently in Mexico, Asia and Russia. Despite exchange controls, the currency depreciated twofold within a year, and continued to slide further in subsequent years (see Figure B1.1).

As a result of the correction, Chile's fiscal position deteriorated. This was largely because of the huge costs of rescuing the banking system, which had collapsed for reasons similar to the Asian banking crises of the late 1990s: a mismatch of currencies and maturities, arising from the pre-crisis perception that the exchange rate was irrevocably fixed; poor supervision; and clear signals that banks in trouble would be bailed out. Links between the banking system and the corporate sector had also increased financial fragility.

Table B1.1 **Chile: economic indicators in the early 1980s**

	1980	1981	1982	1983	1984	1985
GDP growth (%)	7.7	6.7	-13.4	-3.5	6.1	3.5
Inflation (%)	31.2	9.5	20.7	23.1	23.0	26.4
Fiscal surplus (% GDP)	6.1	2.8	-3.4	-2.6	-2.9	-3.7
Gross national savings (% GDP)	13.5	8.0	2.1	4.3	2.8	7.8
Fixed investment (% GDP)	20.9	23.2	15.8	13.7	16.3	17.7
Current Account (% GDP)	-6.9	-14.1	-9.2	-5.5	-10.7	-8.6
Real exchange rate (1986=100)	60.8	52.9	59.0	70.8	74.0	90.9

Source: Central Bank of Chile.

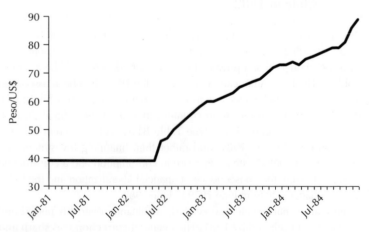

Figure B1.1 Nominal exchange rate in Chile 1981–4

Source: Central Bank of Chile.

1.2 The Bretton Woods institutions

The IMF was established in 1944 to support a global system of exchange rates that were pegged but adjustable. In the post-war world of limited capital mobility, the Fund discharged this function by plugging gaps in countries' balance of payments. It had the capacity to do so because restrictions on capital mobility limited the scale and scope of the requisite interventions. The focus was on whether countries' fiscal and monetary policies were consistent with their exchange rates and, when persistent imbalances developed, on ensuring that the devaluations taken to correct them did not destabilize economic and financial conditions in neighbouring countries.

This was the era in which the Fund developed its distinctive approach to surveillance. Anticipating academic research on the monetary approach to the balance of payments, it formulated the so-called Polak model – named after the founding director of the Fund's research department, Jacques Polak – a parsimonious framework for analysing the balance of payments, which focused on the links between monetary policy, the exchange rate and the current account. The Polak model (described in more detail in Chapter 2) was a fruitful way of analysing a world in which capital flows and the role of expectations could be safely overlooked.

But by the 1990s, overlooking these factors was no longer possible. Financial repression was on the wane, and international capital transactions were gradually – sometimes abruptly – liberalized. Capital account imbalances came to swamp the current account, exposing the limitations of the Polak model and the 'financial programming' approach that Fund staff had constructed around it. That approach paid relatively little attention to the determinants of capital flows: expectations; institutional investors; and the adequacy of prudential supervision and regulation – to cite three now painfully obvious omissions. Correspondingly, IMF conditionality still focused on macroeconomic policies designed to affect the current account, even though the action had increasingly shifted to capital transactions.

It was not that the IMF had failed to change since Bretton Woods. The debt crisis of the 1980s had forced the Fund to recognize the role of private lending to sovereign states. Working with the World Bank, the Fund had contributed to finding a solution to the debt overhang of the developing countries. And with the collapse of communism, the IMF had found yet another role, as adviser to the former Soviet bloc countries undertaking the transition from plan to market. Indeed, the IMF was busy advising the transition economies when the Mexican crisis erupted.

The World Bank too was in flux. In the 1950s and 1960s, its role had been clear. Capital was hard to come by since there was no global capital market on which developing countries could borrow. Private institutions in developed countries were not interested in financing projects in developing countries since there were plenty of low-risk, high-return projects at home. Moreover, the banking and securities industries in the developed countries were heavily regulated. This created a niche for World Bank finance. But as private lending began to pick up, official finance became increasingly irrelevant except for the poorest countries (see Table 1.1).

In response, the Bank has adopted the philosophy that its lending should be done at the market rate. But this means that many developing countries find that World Bank loans are not particularly attractive. As capital markets have become increasingly active, the Bank's *raison d'etre* has been lost. It has responded by branching out into other areas, for example, reinventing itself as a 'knowledge bank', that is, as a technical adviser to developing countries. But the question remains as to why the provision of technical advice should be tied to banking.

The Fund and the Bank have increasingly found themselves trespassing on each other's turf. The former has found that advice on macroeconomic policy is insufficient to remove debt overhangs and rehabilitate developing countries' economic and financial

Table 1.1 **Average annual financial flows to developing countries** (US $ billions)

	Total	Official development assistance	Private
1956–60	21.9	13.2	8.7
1961–70	29.0	16.2	11.5
1971–80	76.6	28.1	38.1
1996	281.6	34.7	246.9

Source: Cuddington (1989) and *Global Economic Prospects* 1998–9, The World Bank.

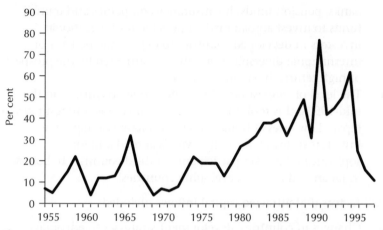

Figure 1.1 Average inflation rate in developing countries
Source: International Finincial Statistics, IMF

prospects. So it has moved to address a wide variety of structural issues that have implications for countries' balance of payments.[1] Meanwhile, the Bank has recognized that structural adjustment and development finance cannot succeed in the absence of a stable macroeconomic environment. So it has grown increasingly concerned with macroeconomics, particularly with the emergence of very serious inflation problems in the developing countries in the 1980s (see Figure 1.1).

In summary, in the 1950s and 1960s, the IMF was the steward of the current account and of an international system of exchange rates that were pegged but adjustable. Today, in contrast, the Fund aspires to become the steward of the capital account. Meanwhile, the mandate and intentions of the World Bank have become increasingly unclear.

1.3 The brave new world of capital mobility

The dramatic increase in capital flows from developed to developing countries reflected the interaction of 'push' factors in the former with 'pull' factors in the latter. There were two prominent push factors :

■   The emergence of a large class of internationally active institutional investors: regulatory changes that permitted banks, pension funds, life insurance companies and mutual funds to invest abroad made it possible for institutional investors in developed countries to exploit the benefits of international diversification. All were attracted by the prospect of high returns in emerging markets.

■ The level of interest rates in the developed countries: in the mid-1990s, this took the form of extremely low interest rates in Japan. Low rates at home made it attractive for Japanese investors to search for higher yields abroad and for sophisticated market participants in third countries to borrow in Japan and lend in developing countries.

Pull factors that attracted capital inflows included:

■ Changes in countries' development strategies to encourage inward foreign direct investment, and rapid privatization by both developing and transition economies (see Table 1.2, which indicates the pattern of reform in Latin America). Many Asian and Latin American countries switched from a development strategy based on import substitution to one based on export promotion. Particularly in Asia, tax subsidies were given to foreign companies willing to invest in strategic export industries.

■ Financial deregulation, which was implemented in a number of countries, partly in response to IMF pressure as the Fund drew lessons from the crises of the 1980s. Some developing countries tried to encourage equity financing of their companies by stimulating the development of stock markets.

■ Much improved macroeconomic policies. The move towards greater price stability in many developing countries improved the economic outlook in places long seen as too dangerous to touch.

For all these reasons, the growth of private capital flows in the 1990s was immense. These flows appeared to contribute to dramatic economic growth in a number of Asian countries, notably Malaysia, Singapore and Taiwan. But that was before the flows changed direction.

Table 1.2 **Latin America: index of reform (1985–95)**

	1985	1986	1987	1988	1989	1990	1991	1992	1993	1994	1995
Trade policy	0.45	0.52	0.63	0.65	0.70	0.76	0.80	0.86	0.88	0.89	0.90
Tax policy	0.40	0.41	0.43	0.45	0.44	0.46	0.45	0.48	0.50	0.52	0.54
Financial	0.45	0.44	0.46	0.45	0.50	0.60	0.66	0.72	0.75	0.75	0.79
Privatization	0.00	0.00	0.00	0.02	0.02	0.04	0.10	0.14	0.18	0.23	0.26
Labour	0.57	0.57	0.57	0.56	0.56	0.56	0.59	0.59	0.59	0.58	0.59
Total	**0.38**	**0.39**	**0.42**	**0.43**	**0.44**	**0.48**	**0.52**	**0.56**	**0.58**	**0.59**	**0.62**

Source: Lora (1997)

Note: the indices are computed for 19 Latin American countries.

1.4 The dark side of capital mobility

1.4.1 Boom and bust cycles

While it may not be true that crises have grown more frequent as capital mobility has increased, we certainly have a different kind of crisis now. New-fangled crises driven by the capital account have replaced old-fashioned crises driven by the current account.

The fact that current account deficits were so large in Mexico and Thailand might suggest that their crises were rooted in the current account. In fact, strong capital inflows masked the problem and made the subsequent crisis that much more devastating. The underlying phenomenon was not new: countries that follow policies designed to enhance growth and stability often have to deal with a boom and bust cycle. At first, capital inflows reward them for their policy probity, fuelling an unprecedented boom. Eventually, however, this happy situation collapses in a panicked withdrawal of funds, triggering a crisis.[2] The reasons may be global – the push factor – or local – the pull factor – but the consequences are fundamentally the same.

On the pull side, capital flows respond to interest rates in the developed countries (see Eichengreen and Mody, 1998). Crises have often followed a marked tightening of monetary conditions in the United States, as happened with Mexico in 1982 and 1994. The Asian currency crises stand out in that they occurred at a time when world interest rates were stable and even falling. This is apparent in Figure 1.2, which shows the US treasury bond rate along with the number of crises in developing countries.[3]

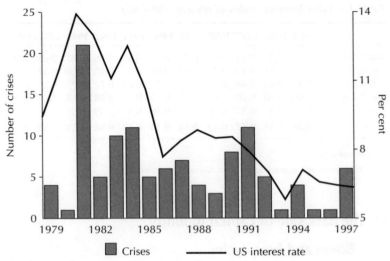

Figure 1.2 Interest rates in the United States and developing country crises (1979–97)

Sources: Interest rate (right scale): *International Financial Statistics*, IMF; number of crises (left scale): Frankel and Rose (1996) and Kraay (1998).

The boom and bust cycle associated with capital flows has been with us for years. It typically occurs when high local interest rates in conjunction with a fixed exchange rate create an irresistible attraction for foreign investors. Non-residents invest in short-term domestic assets, while residents borrow abroad, where interest rates are lower. But the resulting inflow is clearly temporary. While it is admittedly difficult *ex ante* to distinguish temporary from permanent phenomena, especially when the 'temporary' can last for years, it cannot last forever. In particular:

■ Either interest rates will decline as the robustness of the exchange rate anchor is recognized;
■ or the exchange rate will become overvalued as inflows fuel a spending boom and inflation accelerates.

In either case, the inflows will come to an end. The denouement comes in the form of a crisis, be it the Latin American debt suspension of 1982, the expulsion of Italy and the United Kingdom from the European Union's exchange rate mechanism in 1992, Mexico in 1994, Asia in 1997 or Russia in 1998.

Why do governments court this danger? What usually happens is that they regard the exchange rate anchor as a credibility-enhancing commitment, which has worked well to date. Thus, they are typically reluctant to abandon it, especially as they tend to view the inflows as proof that credibility is 'working.' The fixed exchange rate then becomes an aggravating factor because it is a guarantee, freely offered by the monetary authorities, that investors who exit first will not suffer a capital loss.

Countries that maintain a fixed exchange rate in the face of large inflows clearly take on a major risk. Why then do the authorities hesitate to allow the currency to fluctuate more freely while capital inflows are still underway? Their reluctance derives from the fear that competitiveness will suffer if the exchange rate is allowed to appreciate. We return to this dilemma below.

1.4.2 Contagion

Contagion is one of the most troubling aspects of recent financial crises. It was evident in Europe in 1992–3, in Latin America in 1994–5 and in Asia in 1997–8. Surprising connections have emerged, including those running from Asia to Central and Eastern Europe in 1997 and from Russia to Brazil in 1998.

Trade links are the usual explanation for the phenomenon of contagion: a sharp currency depreciation will adversely affect the international competitive position of a country's trading partners, laying their currencies open to speculative attack (see Eichengreen and Rose, 1999; and Glick and Rose, 1998). Thus, contagion can arise even in a financially segmented world. But if that were all of it, one would have expected Korea to be hit shortly after Thailand, not a full six months later. And one would not have expected Brazil to be affected by Korea's devaluation in 1997 or by Russia's devaluation and default in 1998.

'Herd behaviour' by international investors is an important additional cause of contagion. But such behaviour need not imply irrationality (see Box 1.2). Each investor can have good reasons to watch what other investors are doing. For example, the news that other investors are getting out of a market may convey useful information if others have superior knowledge of local market conditions. This phenomenon of 'information cascades' explains why international investors are quick to respond to the news that domestic investors are getting out (see Frankel and Schmukler, 1996).

Box 1.2 **Why it made sense to buy Russian GKOs**

On 17 August 1998, Russia defaulted on its public debt instrument, the GKO. It quickly transpired that a number of highly respected western investors had been caught in the default and were facing huge losses. How could these savvy financiers have gone wrong? Russia's finances were sick – and everyone knew it. Sooner or later, the government would have to do something drastic: either print money or default. In both cases, the rouble would have to depreciate. The markets knew it and they priced Russian bonds accordingly. Yields on GKOs reached a low of 20% in August 1997, but they then started to rise, reaching 300% on 14 August 1998.[1]

Part of the rate is a risk premium, but the rest represents compensation for expected depreciation. Overlooking the risk premium, Figure B1.2 shows the implicit expected rate of devaluation of the rouble against the US dollar (if the risk premium is, say, 10%, this amount should be subtracted) within six months. Quite clearly, from the spring of 1998, the markets expected a very sizeable devaluation, up to 96% on 14 August. The high interest rates received until default represented a down payment in anticipation of a dramatic event. With annual returns of 100%, investors were in fact compensated for the subsequent loss.

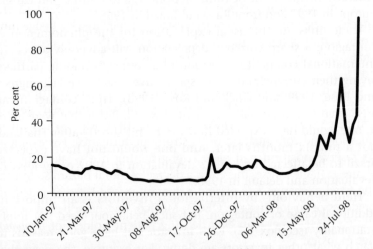

Figure B1.2   Expected devaluation of the rouble

Source: Russian-European Centre for Economic Policy

---

1.   Russians quote an annual rate that is 12 times the monthly rate, a gross approximation that is increasingly misleading as the rate increases. The 'Russian' GKO rate on 14 August was 147.9%.

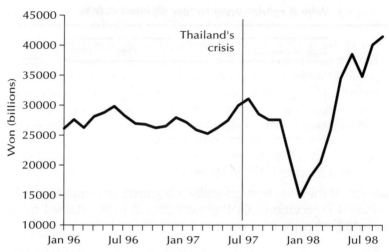

Figure 1.3 Korea: net foreign exchange reserves

Source: International Financial Statistics, IMF.

In addition, the news that other investors are selling an asset conveys information about the balance of supply and demand. If this phenomenon of 'pay-off externalities' is evident in the market's response to news of the distress of the large US hedge fund Long Term Capital Management, why should the reaction to news that other investors were dumping emerging market securities be any different?

Indeed, it is hard to argue that investors were irrational in lending to, say, Korea. The country epitomized the Asian growth 'miracle', and prior to the Thai crisis, there was no reason to question the continuation of its strong performance. For example, its reserve position had been strengthening not weakening (see Figure 1.3). Of course, there was a degree of moral hazard so long as the fixed exchange rate offered a guarantee.[4] And if that failed, its predecessor in joining the OECD, Mexico, had been bailed out by the first IMF super-loan ever, leaving patient holders of *tesobonos* free of losses.

Whatever the channels through which contagion works, the fact that crises can spread has profound implications for international economic policy. The financial crises that result can be devastating. Table 1.3, for example, shows how quickly and deeply expectations can change. It displays growth forecasts for 1997–8 for the Asian countries; these forecasts have swung widely as the depth and

Table 1.3 **Asian countries: growth forecasts from the IMF** (excluding China and India)

Date of Forecast	1996	1997	1998	1999
October 1996[1]	8.0	7.5		
May 1997		7.0	6.7	
October 1997		5.3	5.4	
May 1998			-0.3	3.4
October 1998			-6.0	0.5

Source: World Economic Outlook, IMF.

Note: 1 Includes China and India.

severity of the crisis were gradually recognized. In comparison with pre-crisis expectations, GDP growth forecasts were slashed by an incredible 10 percentage points.

1.4.3 Twin crises

The coincidence of currency crises with banking crises is the single most important reason why developing countries suffer so much deeper recessions than developed countries when their currency pegs collapse. The implication is that it is essential to establish an effective system of bank and financial supervision and regulation before capital flows are liberalized to prevent currency crises from precipitating banking crises.

This has not been the message from the international financial institutions until recently. Why did they fail to recommend it? One conceivable answer is that they hoped that exposure to the rigours of financial integration would impress on reluctant governments the importance of more effective prudential regulation and supervision. But while this gamble may eventually work, the costs can be considerable.

1.5 Evolution and adaptation of the international financial institutions

1.5.1 Tougher challenges

With private capital in abundant supply, the Bretton Woods institutions have lost their leverage. In normal periods, most countries no longer need to rely on them for their financing needs, since they can borrow on attractive terms from commercial banks and on the bond markets. But in times of crisis, this source of funding instantly dries up. When a country comes to the Fund, the volume of financial support required to stabilize the situation is correspondingly greater.

For many years, the rule of thumb for adequate foreign exchange reserves was three months' worth of imports. But in today's world of capital mobility, outstanding balances of short-term liabilities – banks' external liabilities and short-term government bonds – must also be covered by foreign reserves in case investors become reluctant to roll them over. Short-term liabilities are typically much larger than three months' worth of imports. And if residents are inclined to flee in response to developing financial difficulties, the whole of the money supply (M1 or even wider aggregates) has to be covered by foreign reserves to prevent the collapse of the exchange rate regime and the financial system.

Bank runs are a related worry. Because banks tend to be backstopped by the central bank and the government, bank runs create public liabilities. In some cases, even equities have to be protected by the government, as the cases of Hong Kong and Malaysia have shown.   ·

When things go wrong, they can go very wrong. GDP often declines steeply following a devaluation, despite the apparent improvement in international competitiveness associated with the currency's depreciation. All Asian countries experienced sharply negative growth in 1998: Indonesia, -13%; Thailand, -8%; and Korea, -5%. These shifts are dramatic relative to the rapid pace of growth – rates of 6–10% – only a few years earlier.

1.5.2 The IMF

The IMF has attempted to adapt to the reality of large and liquid international capital markets by providing faster, larger and more heavily front-loaded loans. The Mexican support package of February 1995, for example, was unusually large and supplemented by other official donors – the World Bank, the Inter-American Development Bank (IDB) and national governments. The time allowed for decision-making by the IMF's Executive Board was compressed relative to the historical norm.

The IMF's response to the Asian crisis also differed from previous programmes (see Table 1.4). In Thailand in 1997, for example, a new type of support package was introduced: *pari passu* lending by the Japanese Export-Import Bank doubled the amount of IMF support. In Korea, the time from agreement to Board decision was just one day – as opposed to the usual three weeks – and the size of the loan boosted the total to 20 times the country's quota (three-quarters of which was provided through the Fund's newly established Supplemental Reserve Facility).[5] In addition, Korea and Indonesia received 'second lines of defence' from national governments.

IMF lending to the Asian countries was accompanied by traditional macroeconomic conditionality: tight monetary and fiscal policies were initially demanded – though the conditions were eventually relaxed, especially for fiscal policy. IMF conditionality also emphasized structural policies for these countries. This was not a completely new development: ten years ago, Edwards (1989) observed disapprovingly that the IMF was pushing for deeper and more invasive structural conditions. But in Asia, the IMF went further: its conditions included quick bank closures or recapitalization, and breaking up large conglomerates, notably the *chaebol* in Korea.

1.5.3 The World Bank

Meanwhile, the role of the World Bank has shrunk as capital markets have opened and low-income countries have graduated to higher-income ranks. While there is still a role for a development bank for the poorest countries that do not receive private capital inflows, private capital is now abundantly available to medium income countries in non-crisis periods. Countries can find investors for commercially viable projects, either in the form of direct investment or through financial intermediaries. Recently, the Bank has attempted to adapt to this new environment by placing more emphasis on technical assistance, addressing issues like the social safety net, women in development, and environmental protection in developing countries of all income levels. In addition, it now regularly participates in IMF support packages.

Not surprisingly, the demarcation among international financial institutions has been blurred. The IMF now addresses many of the same structural issues as the World Bank and the same financial issues as the Bank for International Settlements (BIS). The World

Table 1.4 IMF programmes in Asia, 1997–8

Country	Dates		Maturity	Amount & sources of funds in US $ billions (see also Table 3.2)	Key Policy Conditions		Second programme
					First programme		
	1st programme	2nd programme			What?	Why?	
Indonesia	5 Nov 1997	15 Jan 1998	36 months	40 (10 IMF, 8 ADB+WB, 22 governments)	Fiscal contraction (target: budget surplus of 1% of GDP)	1. support monetary contraction and defend currency 2. provide for funds to inject into the financial system	1. lower emphasis on bank closures and more comprehensive approach to financial restructuring 2. easing requirements about capital adequacy standards 3. allowed budget deficit = 1% GDP
					Bank closures	3. limit losses of financial institutions 4. signal of serious reforms to restore confidence	
					Enforcement of capital adequacy standards (quick recapitalization of the banks)	Quick return to a solid banking sector	
					Tight domestic credit (money base targets and interest rate floors)	Defend the currency	
					Debt repayments		
					Structural change in the non-financial sector (lower tariffs, opening to foreign direct investment, reducing monopoly powers)		
Korea	4 Dec 1997		36 months	57 (21 IMF, 14 ADB+WB, 22 governments)	Same as Indonesia except: 1. closures focus on merchant banks (no household deposits) rather than commercial banks 2. longer time frame for the enforcement of the capital adequacy standards		Allowed budget deficit = 1% GDP
Thailand	20 Aug 1997	25 Nov 1997	34 months	17.2 (4 IMF, 2.7 ADB+WB, 10.5 governments)	Same as Indonesia		1. lower emphasis on bank closures and more comprehensive approach to financial restructuring 2. easing requirements about capital adequacy standards 3. small budget deficit allowed

Source: Radelet and Sachs (1998)
Note: ADB= Asian Development Bank, IMF= International Monetary Fund, WB= World Bank.

Bank, for its part, has become increasingly involved in macro-economic support, especially at times of crisis when market access is suspended. This too is a reflection of the fact that international payments imbalances are now dominated by capital flows mediated by commercial banks and other institutions. As a result, currency and banking crises tend to come together. Given the Bank's traditional responsibility for providing financial and technical support for bank rehabilitation, it is not surprising that it has increasingly contributed to IMF packages assembled in response to banking crises.

That said, the difficulty of telling the two sides of Washington DC's 19th Street apart raises issues of coordination between the Bretton Woods twins, and between them and other international financial institutions. An obvious worry is inconsistencies in the conditions demanded by the various institutions. Moreover, having the Bank augment IMF support packages complicates the Bank's image with potential recipients and may create difficulties in future negotiations. The Bank's independence may be jeopardized if it is regularly used to overcome the Fund's lending limits and augment its financial resources. Finally, there is an impression that the recent 'coordination' between the Fund and the Bank has been orchestrated under the direction of the larger countries. Transparency and accountability do not benefit from even the appearance of back room deals.

1.6 The IMF: staff and governance

1.6.1 The staff

The IMF has assembled a substantial cadre of economists. Its researchers have been at the forefront of analytical work on applied international economics for years. Its mission chiefs and resident representatives are comparable in quality to the best local economists.

But the hierarchical structure of the Fund is narrow at the top. Ascending through the ranks is difficult. As in any bureaucracy, the system rewards those who 'internalize' the corporate culture. Some would say that this was evident in the Fund's response to the Asian crisis, when tried and true policies were pursued even though the crisis was, in important respects, fundamentally new.

Furthermore, theoretical macroeconomics has undergone several revolutions over the last 25 years, as applied economists have developed theories founded in microeconomics and concepts like rational expectations, time-consistency and credibility. While there are prominent exceptions to the rule, a strongly hierarchical system relying on internal promotion leads to an organization dominated by individuals whose formal training predates the diffusion of these principles.

Finally, lessons from the wealth of experiments witnessed – even designed – by IMF staff have not been fully exploited. While a positive aspect of the IMF's internal organization is the mobility of staff between departments, this mobility declines as staff members climb the ladder. As a result, ideas and experiences do not travel well between departments.

1.6.2 **Governance**

Oversight of the IMF is exercised by the Interim Committee, which meets twice a year and includes the finance ministers from 24 countries. Final authority rests with the Board of Governors: the 182 finance ministers or heads of central banks. Day-to-day decisions, including approval of stand-by agreements and surveillance, are taken by the Executive Directors in Board meetings. These meetings typically take place three times a week.

The Executive Board is responsible for conducting the business of the Fund and exercising the powers delegated to it by the Board of Governors. Unlike the United Nations, where one country has one vote, voting powers at the IMF and the World Bank roughly reflect differences in the economic size and power of member countries.

The Board consists of 24 Executive Directors, of whom 8 represent a single constituency: China, France, Germany, Japan, Russia, Saudi Arabia, the United Kingdom and the United States. According to the Articles of Agreement on which the IMF is founded, decisions are taken by majority unless otherwise specified (Art. XII.5.c; see Box 4.1). The Managing Director presides over the Executive Board but has no vote except when there is an equal division. But decisions are usually made by consensus, with explicit votes rarely taken. In practice, the views of large contributors are important in considering policy changes or dealing with unprecedented situations.

Votes are proportional to quotas, which represent a country's 'weight' in the world economy.[6] The quotas are negotiated when a country joins the IMF and readjusted every five years. (The latest revision took place in February 1999). Importantly, key decisions require 85% of the votes. According to the IMF, 'a member's quota is largely determined by its position relative to other members. A variety of economic factors is considered in determining quotas. The specific formulas used in the calculations have evolved – typically using data on members' GNP, current account transactions and official reserves.'

How well do current quotas and voting shares reflect countries' place in the world economy? The first column in Table 1.5 shows the voting shares of the top 20 countries. The next two columns show the share of each country in world GNP (adjusted for purchasing power) and international trade. Thus, for example, based on GNP, the United States is under-represented in the Fund and is over-represented on the basis of trade.

To provide a crude measure of over- or under-representation, we have looked at the systematic link between a country's votes and the two characteristics (shares in world trade and in world GNP).[7] The results are reported in the last column, which displays the difference between a country's current voting share and the voting share that would follow from applying the same rule to every country. A positive entry indicates over-representation (for example, the United States' actual share exceeds by 1.1 percentage points its 'predicted' share, that is, it 'should' be 16.4% instead of 17.5%), while a negative entry signals under-representation.

According to our calculations, China, Italy, Mexico and Spain are clearly under-represented, while Australia, India, Russia, Saudi Arabia and Venezuela are over-represented.[8] Among the big countries, the United States is over-represented, while Germany and Japan are under-represented. Yet there are no glaring cases of mis-representation among the largest shareholders.

One explanation for over- and under-representation is that the formula used to update the quota tends to carry over from past arrangements: 75% of the existing quota is protected in quota revision, while only 25% is reallocated. This means that those countries that used to be disproportionately important in the world economy tend to be over-represented, while countries that have experienced recent rapid economic growth and are growing in

Table 1.5 **Actual and predicted share of votes in the IMF Board**
(percentage, 20 largest countries)

Country	Vote share 1999	GNP (PPP) share 1997	Trade share 1997	Over (+) or Under (-) representation
United States	17.5	20.8	13.7	1.1
Japan	6.3	8.0	6.9	-1.1
Germany	6.1	4.7	8.9	-1.4
France	5.1	3.5	5.3	0.4
United Kingdom	5.1	3.3	5.2	0.5
Italy	3.3	3.1	4.4	-0.6
Saudi Arabia	3.3	0.3	0.8	2.7
Canada	3.0	1.8	3.4	0.2
Russia	2.8	1.7	1.4	1.5
Netherlands	2.4	0.2	3.2	0.3
China	2.2	11.9	2.5	-1.6
Belgium	2.2	0.6	2.8	0.1
India	2.0	4.3	0.7	1.7
Switzerland	1.6	0.5	1.7	0.3
Australia	1.5	1.0	1.2	0.4
Spain	1.4	1.7	2.2	-0.6
Brazil	1.4	2.8	0.9	0.1
Venezuela	1.3	0.5	0.3	0.9
Mexico	1.2	2.1	1.6	-0.4
Sweden	1.1	0.5	1.4	0.0

Source: IMF and calculations based on World Bank, *World Development Report 1998–9.*

importance, such as China, Korea and Thailand, tend to be under-represented.

1.6.3 An outdated system?

Each of the three weekly Executive Board meetings (with additional meetings scheduled when the Managing Director feels the need) is organized around an agenda based on reports prepared by the staff (from so-called Article IV consultations, programmes, special issues, etc.). A massive amount of detail and documentation is involved. As a result, some national authorities feel that the Directors are not easily controlled, while Directors for their part feel overwhelmed by the staff. Member countries tend to focus only on issues of direct interest to them and provide limited guidance to their representatives.

The Interim Committee is small enough to provide effective control, in contrast to the full Board of Governors. But its composition is heavily tilted towards the developed countries. In many respects, the governance of the IMF still reflects the world of Bretton Woods, when the United States was the dominant economic power, Europe and Japan were its junior partners and many of today's countries were colonies. The Fund's current and future clients, the developing countries, are minority shareholders with little say. This contrasts with the 1950s and 1960s when the countries that were likely to receive assistance dominated IMF decision-making. (Recall, for example, IMF programmes in Italy in 1964 and the United Kingdom in 1967.)

Shareholding based on quotas that are slow to change tends to perpetuate pre-existing patterns of behaviour. The justification is that the major shareholders provide the resources and are therefore entitled to corresponding control. This is a strong argument but one that leaves an uneasy feeling that IMF programmes are not necessarily tailored in a way that maximizes the benefits for the countries to which they apply.

The developing countries would probably be ready to increase their quotas by large amounts, both to enlarge their access to IMF loans and to increase their voting shares to reflect their new status of 'most likely customers'. The current large shareholders are only really active in cases where they see a direct interest. This leaves the IMF staff shaping day-to-day decisions while opening the door to occasional, politically-motivated interference by the large shareholders. The result is that the Board lacks responsibility and the Fund is not in practice accountable to the Interim Committee.

1.7 Whither the IMF?

The IMF has adapted to the new world of capital mobility but not sufficiently to deal with today's high-tech financial crises. The next three chapters examine what remains to be done to make that adaptation complete.

Chapter 2 focuses on crisis prevention. In an ideal world, the IMF would ensure that crises do not occur. But even if this is unrealistic, crises can still be made less frequent, less violent and better foreseen. The official approach since Mexico has been to call for more transparency on the part of borrowers and lenders and for improved provision of information by governments. While this is desirable, we argue that it is unlikely to take us very far. Forecasting crises is like forecasting earthquakes: both are products of complex non-linear systems. While improved prediction is desirable, the prospects for progress on creating 'early warning indicators' should not be overstated.

At the same time, it is possible to reduce the incidence of crises by ensuring that capital liberalization does not run ahead of the ability of developing countries to link into the world financial markets. It is also necessary to adopt exchange rate regimes that are robust enough to cope with sharp capital flow reversals. This generally means more flexibility, even though extreme fixed exchange rate arrangements, such as currency boards and dollarization or euro-ization, will also have a place in the twenty-first century. Chapter 2 explores some of these issues and the role of the IMF during 'peacetime' – when crises are not happening.

Chapter 3 accepts that crises will occur and examines what can be done to limit their destructive effects. Starting from the observation that many recent crises resulted less than their predecessors from macroeconomic problems, we argue that standard IMF responses may no longer work. We take a critical view of the Fund's recent tendencies to increase loan size and to view itself as an international 'lender of last resort'.

Chapter 4 turns to the legitimacy, accountability and transparency of the IMF. Although it has made considerable progress of late, the IMF is still hardly a model of transparency. Its governance structure is muddled, inefficient and susceptible to capture. We argue for fundamental reforms to create a truly independent and accountable IMF. We suggest amending the Articles of Agreement to enhance the independence of the Executive Board, as a way of creating an IMF that is independent of parochial political pressures. We also propose reforming the Interim Committee, creating a body to which the Executive Board is truly accountable.

2 The IMF and Crisis Prevention

The most successful police department is not the one that arrests the most criminals but the one that most dramatically cuts the crime rate. When a house is broken into, the police must respond to the homeowner's call, attempt to track down the burglar and take him into custody. But preventing the burglary in the first place is much better.

The same is true of the IMF. Responding when called to the scene of a crisis is unavoidable, but crisis prevention is far more desirable. Crisis prevention starts with surveillance, which is chiefly conducted as part of the IMF's Article IV consultations, the systematic and regular reviews of each member country – the equivalent of security checks and the neighbourhood patrol for the police department. This chapter reviews how the Fund undertakes this essential task of surveillance. Can the IMF anticipate problems and identify their source, like a police officer on the lookout for suspicious characters?

Each crisis has seen the IMF expand both the size of its interventions and its role. There are regular suggestions that it should go further. The IMF has been encouraged to develop its prevention activities by attempting to foresee crises, improving the flow and quality of information, and acting as a lender of last resort. But why should the IMF be given the responsibility of forecasting crises when rating agencies and private analysts – the financial markets' 'private security guards' – are handsomely rewarded for anticipating the same events? In particular, can the Fund warn a country that it is running the risk of a crisis without precipitating the very event that it wishes to avoid? And what about its new Contingent Credit Lines (CCL) facility?

This chapter also examines a number of new areas of IMF intervention, including its controversial structural policies. It concludes by looking at who surveys and whom is surveyed, detecting a growing imbalance as the rich countries leave the dangerous neighbourhoods now mostly populated by emerging markets.

2.1 Surveillance and financial programming

Surveillance is at the heart of the Fund's activities. It is structured around the Article IV consultations, which for most countries take place every year, though in some cases every two years. Little is known about these consultations outside the Fund. Indeed, it is only recently that the document written in preparation for each country's review, the Recent Economic Developments (REDs) report, has been released when governments agree. Even so, the other key document, the Staff Report, remains largely confidential. Although the Fund has recently decided on a pilot programme of releasing Staff Reports, again the country's authorization is needed: so far only five small countries have agreed – Albania, Aruba, Estonia, Malta and Trinidad and Tobago.

Each consultation is followed by a deliberation by the Executive Board, giving rise to a short discussion in the Fund's Annual Report. Given the large number of countries in the Fund's membership, it is unlikely that the Board exercises close scrutiny in each and every case, which raises questions about effectiveness and accountability.

2.1.1 Has financial programming outlived its usefulness?

The Fund's basic approach to crisis management continues to derive from an accounting framework known as 'financial programming', an approach based on the model enshrined in Polak (1957).[9] Changes in a country's international reserves are seen as the outcome of a mismatch between money supply and money demand. The normal assumption is that most mismatches are driven by an excessive supply of domestic credit. According to this view, correcting external imbalances requires a cut in central bank credit growth. Particular attention is paid to fiscal policy and monetary financing of budget deficits, and reducing the deficit is typically the recommended means of reducing excessive credit growth.

The simplicity of the Polak model is its strength. Indeed, reviewing its role 40 years later, Polak (1997) argued that the model has endured so long because of the parsimony of its underlying logic and because it relies on well-known and long-established relationships: money demand and the link between imports and GDP. Polak further argues that the many extensions to the model that have been proposed would have to be based on what he sees as tenuous links: for example, those between capital movements, interest rate and exchange rate expectations; the response of interest rates to budget imbalances; and the effect of the exchange rate on inflationary expectations.

A full critique of the Polak model was offered a decade ago by Edwards (1989). Reviewing the evolution of knowledge in macroeconomics since the late 1950s, Edwards claimed that important improvements in our understanding of the key macroeconomic relationships had been downplayed or even ignored by the Fund: 'There is an urgent need to seriously revise this framework, incorporating the most important developments in the theory of economic policy that have taken place in the last 15 years or so.'

Polak's response (1997) was unrepentant: 'It is true that ever since the mid-1970s econometricians inside and outside the Fund have made valuable efforts to build more elaborate models. The insights provided by these papers did not, however, have a significant effect on the programming activities of the organization. For programme design as well as control, the Fund has continued to use a simple model, with a very limited number of standard variables, subject to an elaboration on an *ad hoc* basis.'

With the hindsight provided by recent crises, this defence of simplicity and 'ad hockery' is hard to swallow. Edwards' critique (1989) provides a detailed list of the many changes in our theoretical and empirical knowledge that have invalidated the IMF's financial programming. The most important changes include the role of expectations, the influence of financial markets and the view that not all budget and current account deficits are bad.

Importantly for IMF programmes, our understanding of credibility has deepened: we now know that a strategy that seems to be the best today will not be equally desirable later on – partly because conditions inevitably change and partly because of the successful effects of the strategy itself. This is known as the time-inconsistency problem. Changing course may be misinterpreted as a relapse into unsustainable policies: credibility is precious and regaining it once it is lost can be enormously costly.

But rigidly upholding previous commitments is not always the proper response. Under certain circumstances, the solution may be to adopt a strategy that is less exacting initially but more enduring – in other words, a credible, time-consistent strategy. The frequent 'adjustments' to IMF programmes (for example, the conditions applied to Korea in 1997–8, which repeatedly changed over the first six months) suggest that this lesson has not yet been fully incorporated into the Fund's financial programming.

Capital markets too have changed. The lifting of restrictions on capital transactions has fuelled the explosive growth of capital flows. The idea that balance of payments deficits are inevitably rooted in current account deficits that result from fiscal irresponsibility is archaic in a world where trade and debt service can be swamped by capital flows. Financial programming underestimates the role of banking and finance.

Yet financial programming is a well-oiled machinery, which still frames the IMF's mode of operation, from Article IV consultations to emergency interventions. For decades, it has provided most of the right answers. But it has evolved into a procedure that increasingly constrains creative thinking and provides a false sense of security. In a world where the list of fundamental weaknesses grows with each jolt to financial markets, there is no substitute for an approach that pulls together various strands of analysis and looks for clues outside the narrow confines of the Polak model. Financial markets have moved a long way in speed and sophistication; the Fund has no choice but to move along with them.

2.2 The Fund's stand on policy prescription

As part of its surveillance activity, the Fund faces a number of recurrent questions: when and how should member countries liberalize their capital accounts? What is the best exchange rate regime? And should the standards used in developed countries be applied in developing countries and emerging markets? Here we ask whether the Fund should take a position on these crucial issues, and if so, which one.

2.2.1 Capital account liberalization

There is no question that countries benefit from trade liberalization. But in contrast with free trade, capital mobility may not be healthy for each and every country. Without deep, efficient and mature domestic capital markets, capital flows may be highly disruptive.

Over the last decade and a half, the IMF has promoted the liberalization of capital flows. This clearly reflects the thinking of its principal shareholders. In particular, the US government has been pushing for capital account convertibility in almost every international forum.[10] Korea is a particularly unsettling example of the problems to which this can lead: as a pre-condition of OECD membership, Korea was required to open its capital account, and a devastating crisis followed.

The IMF's enthusiasm for unconditional capital liberalization has dimmed a little recently. Yet at the annual meetings in Hong Kong in September 1997, the Interim Committee asked the Executive Board to consider revisions of the Articles of Agreement that would formally recognize capital account liberalization as one of the Fund's objectives and extend IMF jurisdiction to capital movements.

In fact, there is not a strong case for the full removal of capital controls while weaknesses in domestic financial systems persist. Even if the IMF now claims that it can exercise its new mandate to urge restraint from premature liberalization, it is not clear why the mandate is needed in the first place. After all, the Fund has always discussed such issues with its member countries.

In principle, capital mobility can have many positive effects, especially in hitherto financially repressed developing countries:

■ Capital mobility promotes the efficient allocation of productive activities around the world, and portfolio diversification allows stable consumption. Both mechanisms should stimulate growth and improve welfare.

■ International investors monitor economic policies and impose discipline.

■ Capital account opening can spur the development of domestic financial markets.

In practice, however, the magnitude of these effects is uncertain. Estimates of the growth dividend from capital account liberalization range from the optimistic (between 2–5% of GDP, according to van Wincoop, 1994) to the sceptical (Rodrik, 1998, who finds 'no evidence that countries without capital controls would have grown faster, invested more or experienced lower inflation'). More importantly, in contrast with trade liberalization, capital account liberalization is known to introduce distortions because of the widespread presence of information asymmetries in financial markets. This is precisely why, in most countries, financial markets are tightly regulated and supervised. Calls for more rigorous regulation are, if anything, growing louder.

It is true that some governments retain capital controls to enforce financial repression and delay reforms without facing the disciplinary pressure of open financial markets. But using capital account opening as a device to push reluctant governments towards better policies is a dangerous gamble. The combination of half-hearted opening and market-unfriendly policies often results in crisis, as Asia and Russia have demonstrated. A crisis may be what is needed to trigger a change in policy but its costs can be overwhelming.

Indeed, financial opening has often been followed by financial crisis. Latin America in the early 1980s provides a good example (see Box 2.1). This experience, the predecessor of the Asian banking crises, highlights the importance of properly phasing in domestic, and especially international, financial liberalization.

Capital flows can be volatile, exaggerating the business cycle and increasing the chances of financial crisis. In poorly regulated markets, external borrowing tends to be short-term and denominated in foreign currencies, while domestic lending is long-term and in the domestic currency. Moral hazard occurs when investors are led to believe that the exchange rate will be defended and that, in the event of crisis, they will be rescued because they – or the borrowing country – are 'too big to fail'. Markets operate on the assumption that fear for a country losing market access will prevent default, irrespective of the costs. What can be done?

The first answer is to strengthen financial supervision, and the logical place to start is with adoption of the Basle Core Principles and the IMF's Framework for Financial Stability.[11] Until a sound domestic financial system is established, there is no case for full removal of capital controls. Countries that lack appropriate financial supervision and means to enforce sound banking may

Box 2.1 **The dangers of financial liberalization: evidence from Latin America**

Argentina and Chile liberalized their financial systems in the late 1970s and early 1980s and also allowed large inflows of capital, mainly in the form of external debt. Figure B2.1 shows the rapid response of bank credit, which increased threefold in the following five years. In each case, the result was a severe banking crisis. The clean-up costs were staggering, estimated at about 13% of GDP in Argentina and 20% in Chile (see Table 2.1 on page 33). In contrast, Colombia followed a much more prudent approach when liberalizing its banking system. It experienced a very moderate increase in lending through the same period and avoided the crisis that swept through much of Latin America in the 1980s.

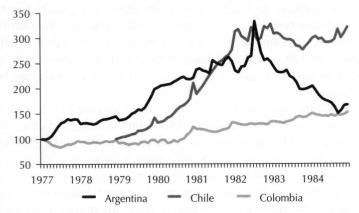

Figure B2.1 Real bank credit to the private sector (Index=100 at begining of sample)

Source: IFS line 22d (claims from private banking systems to no-banking private sector) and CPI.

Systematic analysis of financial intermediation and macroeconomic performance in Latin America shows a strong negative correlation between financial intermediation and growth during the 1970s and 1980s (De Gregorio and Guidotti, 1995). The absence of adequate regulation, combined with the expectation that governments will intervene in a financial crisis, leads to overlending by banks and a loss of efficiency in the allocation of funds. While financial development generally improves a country's growth performance, the Latin American experience of the 1970s and 1980s shows that hasty liberalization followed by a crisis can prove very costly, setting back economic growth considerably.

Box 2.2 **The Chilean experience with capital controls**

Chile's unremunerated reserve requirement (URR) on most capital inflows – the *encaje* – is a market-based and non-discriminatory form of capital control with many desirable macroeconomic effects. It may well have softened the impact of the financial turmoil of 1998. The specifics of the reserve requirement have changed over time, but from 1992–8, 30% of most inflows had to be deposited, with no interest, at the central bank for a one-year period. This represents a fixed cost of entry, which is more severe the shorter the period the inflow stays in Chile.[1] While the effects on the interest and exchange rates are ambiguous and probably small and short-lived (see Edwards, 1998a; and De Gregorio, Edwards and Valdés, 1999), the *encaje* discourages the entry of hot money without reducing overall capital inflows. It also promotes a lengthening of the maturity of inflows, as Table B2.1 confirms. Among the emerging markets, Chile's share of short-term debt in total debt is one of the smallest.

Table B2.1 **Chile's external debt** (US$ millions)

	1990	1991	1992	1993	1994	1995	1996	1997	1998
Total external debt	17425	16364	18242	19186	21478	21736	22979	26701	31546
Private	5633	5810	8619	10166	12343	14235	17816	21613	25489
Public	11792	10554	9623	9020	9135	7501	5163	5088	5697
Long- & medium-term	14043	14165	14767	15699	17613	18305	20344	25414	29946
Short-term	3382	2199	3475	3487	3865	3431	2635	1287	1600
Short-term/Total (%)	19.4	13.4	19.0	18.2	18.0	15.8	11.5	4.8	5.1

Source: Central Bank of Chile.

Chile's approach may not be transferable to every country. For a start, the economy already had strong fundamentals when the *encaje* was introduced. In addition, Chile has one of the lowest levels of corruption among developing countries, an important consideration for the administration of controls.

Neither is the *encaje* without adverse side effects. Small and medium-size firms without access to long-term international finance have to pay high domestic interest rates. Policy-makers may rely too heavily on controls and pursue risky monetary and fiscal policies in the erroneous belief that they have very limited effects on the real exchange rate or the capital account.

---

1. Calculations by De Gregorio, Edwards and Valdés (1999) indicate that for a LIBOR of 6%, the URR is equivalent to an additional annual financial cost of 23% for operations covering a one-month holding period, 8% at three months, and 1% at two years. For a description and discussion of the evidence, see Nadal de Simone and Sorsa (1999).

still make progress by adopting the intermediate step of shifting from administrative controls to market-based restrictions of the Chilean type, as described in Box 2.2.

The second answer is to adopt an adapted exchange rate regime, an issue to which we now turn.

2.2.2 **Implications for exchange rate policy**

Since the Jamaica agreements of 1976, the IMF has not had an official view on its member countries' exchange rate regimes. But can it completely detach itself from this perennial source of controversy? Speculative attacks on currencies cannot occur unless monetary authorities resist exchange rate movements and, in the process, offer one-way bets. Currently, about half of the Fund's member countries declare a fixed parity, presumably readying themselves for an attack. Why does the Fund not encourage them more forcefully to move out of the firing range by introducing at least some degree of flexibility?

Apparently, the Fund agrees with the view that a fixed exchange rate regime allows a country to impose monetary discipline on itself. And there have been some noticeable successes with exchange-rate-based disinflations: Argentina, Bolivia, Brazil, France, Israel, Italy and Russia are some of the many countries that have anchored their disinflation policies on a fixed exchange rate (Fischer etal., 1999, presents a comprehensive review). But the trick is to disinflate and then dispose of the time bomb that is ticking away in any fixed exchange rate regime.

The sad experience with exit policies – moving to a flexible exchange rate regime and abandoning the fixed rate – is that policy-makers always want to disinflate just a little bit more. They are reluctant to abandon a strategy that has worked well, and they tend to think that crises only affect other countries. They are also wary of being misunderstood by the markets and of losing their hard-won credibility. Tomorrow is always the right time to float. Yet time and again, crises hit suddenly, and the costs, when accompanied by a banking crisis, can be enormous (see Table 2.1).

Should the IMF recommend exchange rate flexibility?[12] In general, yes. But the recommendation is being held up by three main considerations:

Table 2.1 **Costs of bank restructuring: some examples**

Banking Crisis	Cost as percentage of GDP
Argentina, 1982	13.0
Chile, 1981	19.6
Finland, 1991	8.2
Norway, 1988	4.5
Sweden ,1991	4.5
Venezuela, 1994	8.2

Sources: Rojas-Suβrez and Weisbrod (1996); and World Bank (1997).

- First, flexibility works well if the foreign exchange market is well-developed. In particular, an interbank foreign exchange market has to be developed with the backing of a domestic financial market, the availability of instruments that can protect against haphazard fluctuations and the associated know-how.
- Second, moving to a floating rate regime is fraught with dangers if the markets misconstrue a shift to flexibility as a signal that monetary discipline is being jettisoned.
- Third, giving advice means taking responsibility. Like any institution, the IMF cares about its own reputation: it does not want to be seen as advocating a significant policy shift that may fail for reasons beyond its direct control.
- Finally, exchange rate flexibility is no panacea. Freely floating exchange rates are known to exhibit wide fluctuations, which can give rise to economic and political dislocations. This is why the tightly-integrated countries of the European Union have always wanted to keep a level playing field for their common market by managing a system of fixed exchange rates, a goal they have sought to advance recently by moving to monetary union.

The truth is that there is no universal answer. But what has become clear is that pegged exchange rates are an invitation to crisis. For countries with good reasons to attempt to minimize fluctuations – because of trade integration or anti-inflationary discipline – there are two ways out: dirty floating or a currency board. Dirty floating removes the one-way bet from the market while currency boards provide enough commitment to reduce the risk of speculative attacks. But the latter are not fail-safe: Argentina and Hong Kong have undergone repeated attacks in recent years. Nor are they without costs, as recessions in Argentina in 1995 and 1999 make clear.

Dollarization or euro-ization on the other hand, are fail-safe policies since there is no currency to attack. But there are serious drawbacks, the main ones being the political significance of giving up the national currency and the complete loss of seigniorage.[13] And such arrangements come with the same costs as currency boards: loss of monetary policy and the function of lender of last resort. But they also have the same discipline benefit as currency boards though they are more credible and eliminate the currency risk premium. This does not mean that dollarization or euro-ization is always an acceptable way of adopting a fixed exchange rate. Countries that need to undergo important relative price changes (for example, the transition economies) or that are open to frequent external shocks (for example, primary commodity exporters) may find the cost of an irremediably fixed exchange rate too costly at times.

Another suggested element of a country's exchange rate policy is that both the public and private sectors should build up foreign currency reserves. Proponents of this approach (for example, Feldstein, 1999) argue that amassing large amounts of liquidity is a credible deterrent to speculative attacks. The Achilles' heel of a fixed exchange rate regime is that the authorities are prevented from bailing out private banks and financial institutions through money creation or deficit financing, making an interest-rate defence of the currency nearly always self-defeating.

Accumulating large amounts of foreign currency liquidity is meant to counter this weakness. That is certainly the conclusion the Argentine authorities have drawn from the speculative attacks against their currency board. But there are reasons to question whether the approach is fail-safe. To start with, even a large quantity of reserves does not buy much in a world of immensely liquid markets. In addition, for this strategy to work as a deterrent, the size of the stockpile must be widely known. There is a danger that banks will engage in dynamic hedging and accumulate even larger liabilities as a result of the implicit guarantee thus offered to them, as seems to have happened in Argentina. Finally, such reserves are idle resources.

Even if the IMF were to become an active promoter of exchange rate flexibility, it would have to answer the next question: what should be the rule for monetary policy once the exchange rate anchor is lost? The Fund has recently advocated inflation targets for Brazil, joining a bandwagon set rolling in New Zealand a decade ago. But inflation targeting has not been fully tested in developed economies and it is virtually untried in developing countries. Adopting this approach is unusual for an institution that has often been slow to respond positively to new developments.

2.2.3 Financial market supervision and regulation

Financial market supervision and regulation play a fundamental role in limiting the risk of a domestic meltdown and making financial markets and institutions better able to cope with shocks, whether they originate locally or are transmitted from abroad. National supervisors and regulators clearly enjoy an information advantage over international institutions so it makes sense to keep this activity at the national level. But once the capital account is liberalized and national markets become interconnected, two difficulties arise:

■ An externality, as poor supervision and regulation in one country can trigger contagious crises elsewhere.

■ Moral hazard, as national supervisors and regulators may gamble that a soft approach enhances market competitiveness and that an international bail-out will be forthcoming in the event of a major crisis.

These risks have long been recognized among the developed countries, and this is what led to the setting up of the Basle Committee on Banking Supervision. This committee has adopted capital standards designed for banks in the developed countries. In response to the Mexican crisis, the BIS and the IMF have recognized the need to develop standards for banks in developing countries. As more countries become emerging markets, the approach needs to be widened and deepened.

When the IMF takes the initiative of promoting capital account liberalization, it must take responsibility for warning about the risks of financial fragility and promote adequate measures, guiding developing countries through the sequence of supervision and regulation measures that will smooth transition to open financial markets. The ideal is that all countries are brought up to the standards of international best practice, but this takes time. Two short-cuts are possible:

- First, set international standards. This is in line with the Basle Core Principles, but their implementation often proves to be a serious problem.
- Second, open the domestic market to foreign institutions that are subject to better home country supervision. But when this strategy is politically difficult, it may provoke a backlash.

In the end, the presence of a serious externality, most visible in the event of contagion, requires some degree of international cooperation. National regulators cannot simply be left alone, nor must the principles be universal for each and every market irrespective of its stage of development. So if some international surveillance is called for, should the IMF do it?

In many ways, this question is similar to the issue of regulation at the national level: should the central bank also be the regulator and supervisor of banks and financial institutions? Increasingly, the answer is no, primarily because of a conflict of interest: if a central bank fails in the regulatory and supervisory function, it is in a weak position to refuse to bail out failed institutions. The Basle Committee on Banking Supervision is in place and has accumulated experience. Initially set up by the rich countries, it now needs to become universal and propose standards that the IMF can use as part of its surveillance procedure, building on the Financial Stability Forum set up following the Asian crisis.[14]

2.3 Can crises be foreseen? Can the IMF do the job?

2.3.1 The analytics of predicting currency crises[15]

Concern about the disruptive effects of currency and banking crises has led to many attempts at prediction.[16] Yet this enterprise – and policies that depend on our ability to make accurate predictions – is subject to important criticisms.

For a start, not all crises are alike. They defy generalization and complicate efforts at prediction. Years of research have identified the macroeconomic fundamentals – excessively expansionary monetary and fiscal policies, real exchange rate overvaluation, etc. – traditionally associated with a speculative attack and the exhaustion of currency reserves. Following the Mexican crisis, the focus shifted from traditional macroeconomic fundamentals to the maturity structure and currency composition of short-term government debt. After the Asian crisis, the focus shifted again.

It is now recognized that macroeconomic and even financial fundamentals do not tell the entire story. Equally important can be a government's willingness to defend the currency. Governments trade off the immediate costs of defending the current exchange rate against the longer term benefits of enhanced credibility. Whether justified by a concern with external competitiveness or not, an attack can tip the balance of costs and benefits towards giving up on the existing parity. The emphasis then shifts to domestic economic or political weaknesses, which can sap a government's resolve to defend the currency when its financial commitments are threatened. Those weaknesses, in turn, render currencies vulnerable to attack.

What makes it costly for a government to defend a currency peg or, alternatively, to abandon the peg is uncertainty about the peg's appropriateness and uncertainty about the timing of an attack that leads to a crisis. The reasons for a crisis vary from country to country and shift over time. For example:

■ The European crisis of 1992–3 demonstrated the role of high unemployment and weak economic growth.

■ In Mexico in 1994–5 and earlier elsewhere in Latin America, a fragile banking system combined with fiscal deficits financed by short-term capital inflows proved to be a sure formula for a currency crisis.

■ In Asia, Thailand suffered first from exhausting its foreign reserves in forward off-balance sheet transactions, and then from the weak condition of its banking system. These problems with Thailand's international competitiveness were sufficiently evident that the IMF had warned the government well before its currency devaluation of July 1997. Indonesia and Korea, which had better macroeconomic fundamentals, were not forewarned by the IMF before their currencies started to fall sharply in December 1997. Although high short-term debt relative to foreign reserves was a common factor in the three countries, this variable was not added to the list of early warning indicators until after the crises.

Future crises will no doubt add still more items to the list of potential sources of weakness, possibly including excessive property prices, heavily indebted non-financial corporations (especially when the debts are denominated in foreign currencies) and other considerations yet to be pinpointed.

Even when shrewd observers conclude that a currency peg is vulnerable, no single market participant is likely to be large enough to build up the short position in foreign currency forward markets that is needed to exhaust the authorities' reserves. For that to occur, a large number of investors have to coordinate their actions. What serves as a coordinating device is likely to vary from case to case and generally eludes prediction.

For all these reasons, crises will always be difficult to forecast. Box 2.3 offers an illustrative example of the unavoidable technical difficulties involved. And there is an additional reason why early warning indicators cannot be perfected: as soon as a reliable indicator is found, market participants take it into account, changing their behaviour by taking money out one step earlier to avoid being caught in the crisis. The change in behaviour will make an otherwise perfect alarm bell obsolete.[17]

Box 2.3 **The poor performance of crisis indicators**

Examination of attempts to build early warning indicators underscores the difficulties of predicting crises. Much effort has gone into uncovering relationships between observable macroeconomic and financial indicators, with the aim of assessing the probability of large changes in exchange rates and runs on reserves. The relationship tends to be very sensitive to the choice of countries and periods for which the exercise is carried out, which belies the notion that there are a single set of variables and a stable set of relationships on which crisis forecasting can be based.

The models that perform best in statistical terms tend to rely on variables like reversals in the direction of capital flows and sudden reserve losses, which are concurrent rather than leading indicators of currency crises. Once this kind of information is available, it is too late. The same criticism applies to models that rely for their predictive power

continued

Box 2.3 continued

on the number of crises erupting in other countries in the current or immediately preceding months.

Any early warning indicator faces two risks:

- missing out on a crisis that actually occurs – so-called Type I error;
- issuing a warning signal for a crisis that does not occur – Type II error.

In order to reduce Type I errors, the indicator's trigger, the threshold value at which a signal of trouble is issued, has to be made more sensitive. But then the risk is of more frequent Type II errors, that is, issuing many false signals, with dubious overall progress. This can be illustrated with the following simple example where the only crisis indicator is the current account deficit. If a signal is issued each time the deficit exceeds 5% of GDP, many crises will not be detected – for example, Indonesia – and the number of Type I errors may be large. If the trigger is lowered to a deficit of 2% of GDP, there will be many warnings, most of them false alarms, increasing Type II error. There is a trade-off between the two types of error.

Of course, most early warning systems look at more than one indicator. The sensitivity of the trigger is then set by the estimated probability of a crisis. For example, an early warning signal could be triggered whenever the odds of a crisis exceed 50%. Using such a device and re-running history for the developed countries over the period 1959–93, Wyplosz (1998) finds that a crisis signal would have been issued 66 times, always wrongly, and would have missed all 41 crises – 100% Type I error, 5% Type II error.[1]

Moving the probability threshold required to issue a signal to below 50% allows the indicator to spot some crises, but it also increases false alarms. When the threshold is gradually lowered from 50% to a mere 5%, the proportion of both correct and incorrect signals grows as the trigger is made more sensitive. At the lowest threshold, the indicator still only catches 14 of the 41 crises, while issuing no less than 697 erroneous warning signals. Using models as warning indicators may be better than just flipping a coin, but there are still serious difficulties in trying to construct an accurate forecast.

---

1. This study uses similar econometric models to Eichengreen, Rose and Wyplosz (1995) for the OECD countries; and Frankel and Rose (1996) for the emerging markets.

2.3.2 **Can the IMF outperform the market?**

Should the IMF assume the responsibility of issuing crisis warnings? It is true that the IMF routinely assesses the sustainability of balance of payments positions, but rating agencies too are in the business of assessing sovereign borrowers and they already monitor a large number of countries (Box 2.4 briefly considers their performance).

Box 2.4 **The performance of rating agencies**

Strictly speaking, the function of rating agencies is not to assess country or currency risk but to rate the risk of default of a given security. They have performed relatively well in rating private companies, but their track record for sovereign ratings is less impressive. They failed to anticipate both the 1994–5 Mexican crisis and the 1997–8 Asian crisis.

The Japan Center for International Finance (1999) compares rating changes of major agencies. It reports that there was only one instance of downgrading issued for Thailand before the 2 July baht devaluation: Moody's downgrading in April 1997. Even after the devaluation, S&P and Thomson BankWatch did not downgrade until September 1997.

In December 1997, one company suddenly downgraded Korea by three notches, a move partially reversed in January. Fitch IBCA too widely missed the mark and while it acknowledged that its experts were not looking at the right indicators, it pleaded special circumstances: 'There were no early warnings about Korea from us or, to the best of our knowledge, from other market participants.'[1] It further stated: 'Fitch IBCA used to think that a high proportion of short-term debt was a worry only with highly indebted countries, but we now know that short-term debt creates a key vulnerability for any sovereign, even one with relatively low overall debt ratios like Korea.' Standard and Poor's and Moody's did not take any such responsibility, instead blaming the lack of transparency.

Having failed to spot the Asian crisis, rating agencies then downgraded the sovereign debt of the crisis countries. Such a reaction aggravates a bad situation. It can turn a budding crisis into all-out panic. Indeed, many pension funds, mutual funds and several other financial institutions are prevented from holding sub-asset-grade paper. Hence, they are forced to sell a country's debt into a weakening market as soon as an agency downgrades it. In this way, rating agencies may well destabilize the markets.

1. Fitch IBCA (1998) and Fitch IBCA: Credit Agency Accepts Criticism over Asia, Financial Times, 14 January 1998.

Reviewing its own surveillance performance in Asia, the IMF notes: 'the projections of both the Fund and outsiders were revised progressively downward by very large amounts: very few economists foresaw how deep the slumps would be' (Lane et al., 1999). This is not surprising: private and public forecasts tend to be conservative and move together. A private forecasting agency that turns out to be wrong is punished when its forecast is an outlier, not when the forecast is close to the market average. The incentives are for conservative behaviour and following the market. As a result, forecasters tend to herd together and discrepancies are minor.[18]

Technically, both the IMF and private agencies face the same challenges. The difference between them lies in the information they collect and their incentives and responsibilities to their constituencies. In conjunction with its regular surveillance activities, the IMF collects and processes information on all its member countries. It also operates a research department of highly trained economists, who can develop forecasts that are presumably as good as those of any other institution. And as a public institution, the IMF does not have to follow the market. Moreover, it may have better information, as it interacts directly with governments and receives information that is not publicly available.

On the other hand, the IMF faces two serious conflicts of interest:

- First, there is a conflict between duty to its membership and duty to international financial markets. The Fund's influence on member governments relies on sharing private information. Divulging crisis signals based on confidential information from a member government is bound to sour the relationship. For example, for more than a year, the Fund was aware of the severity of Thailand's situation but did not issue public warnings. It now claims that doing so would have unnecessarily antagonized the Thai government.[19]
- Second, there is a conflict between providing relevant information and affecting events. If the IMF issues a warning signal that appears to precipitate a crisis, it could well be blamed for creating the crisis by predicting it.

For all these reasons it is unlikely that the IMF can do better than the market in predicting crises. It should therefore stay away from this inherently difficult task. Private agencies move in a herd and are still in business, but the IMF stands to damage its reputation and its ability to impose conditionality after a crisis as a result of forecasting failures. Furthermore, once a programme is in place, the IMF is invested in the policies' success and cannot act as an impartial judge.

2.3.3 Information dissemination and transparency

Following the Mexican and Asian crises, officials from national governments and international financial institutions like the IMF have emphasized the need for better information. (Mexico, for example, delayed the release of data on its reserves position, keeping investors in the dark.) Indeed, it has become a recurrent theme of G-22 reports and numerous other international studies, and the view is clearly not controversial. If they had been better informed prior to a crisis, the argument goes, international financial institutions as well as market participants would have been able to anticipate the crisis; officials could have completed timely policy adjustments; and the markets could have helped enforce discipline where needed. The conclusion is that due to a lack of transparency in economic data – foreign exchange reserves, monetary aggregates, etc. – there was a dearth of information about the extent of the problem.

But some nuance is needed in this view. In fact, much relevant information is available, but it is provided by different sources and is often contradictory, contributing to a sense of confusion. Thus, there is a role for an institution to gather and disseminate standardized information. This is an international public service that cannot be left entirely to markets. Is the IMF suited for solving this problem?

One argument is that through its own network and contacts with local officials during Article IV consultations, the IMF has better information than private market participants and other public or private institutions. How then can this presumed comparative advantage be put to good use? Following the Mexican crisis, the IMF moved quickly to establish the Special Data Dissemination System (SDDS). It then developed the General Data Dissemination Standard (GDDS), where countries' reports are produced according to agreed standards. Economic information can be obtained with frequent updates and, in some cases, links to national authorities' websites. Currently, 47 countries have signed on but only 17 offer complete reports. To take one telling example, Brazil was not a subscriber to GDDS before its 1998 crisis.

The IMF's most relevant economic information is in the REDs reports produced for Article IV consultations. Until recently, REDs were confidential, but they are now released to the public subject to the agreement of the national authorities. Public Information Notices (PINs) are the Fund's new system of releasing summary information on Article IV Board discussions. Box 2.5 presents recent IMF efforts at transparency. It would be desirable from the point of view of data dissemination for the Fund to publish all REDs without first having to obtain permission from often reluctant member countries. But politics within the Board might also prevent full

Box 2.5 **The IMF's long march towards greater transparency**

The IMF continues to take baby steps in the direction of greater transparency. Executive Directors' assessments of country conditions – or, more precisely, the meeting chairman's (typically, the Managing Director's) summary thereof – formed on the basis of the staff team's Article IV report and other documents, are now released to the Public in the form of Public Information Notices (PINs), subject to the agreement of the country.

On 5 April 1999, the Board agreed to the voluntary release of Article IV staff reports on an experimental basis. Under the terms of this pilot project, countries that volunteer will allow staff reports to be released. This 'closed end' project is to run for 18 months; the Fund plans to begin reviewing experience with it after 12 months.

Finally, the Board has agreed that there should be a presumption that Letters of Intent, Memoranda of Economic and Financial Policies, and Policy Framework Papers, the key documents governing cases where countries actually draw on IMF resources, should also be released to the public.[1] But publication of these documents is not mandatory: a country that feels that programme implementation would be damaged by their disclosure could prevent their release by explaining to the Board the basis for its decision.

---

1. For information on these policies, see 'IMF Takes Additional Steps to Enhance Transparency', PIN 99/36 (16 April 1999), www.imf.org/external/np/sec/pn/1999/PN9936.HTM.

disclosure of information. For this reason, an independent IMF would better fulfil the role of disseminating information. The implications of this argument are developed in Chapter 4.

The IMF's short experience with data dissemination suggests that assembling and publishing relevant data is intrinsically difficult and tends to lag one step behind action. The Fund does not really exploit the comparative advantage that it claims to hold. Why not?

One possible reason is that confidentiality fundamentally clashes with dissemination, rendering the Fund reluctant to reveal what it knows. Another is that there is in fact little that the IMF knows that other interested parties do not: some former staff members who have gone on to work in private financial institutions insist that they now know more and sooner (CEPR, 1998). In addition, conflicts of interest are a serious issue in concentrating data in one agency such as the IMF, which is also involved in policy-making. Yet another reason is that data dissemination is limited to macroeconomic indicators that are more relevant to fundamentals-based crises. Data relevant to liquidity crises, such as private sector external indebtedness, change quickly making timely dissemination nearly impossible.

We conclude that neither more accurate forecasting nor better data guarantee our ability to avoid crises in the future. Nor is it plausible that the IMF is best suited for enhancing transparency. Nevertheless, the IMF can take a stance on the vulnerabilities that should be of concern to its member countries. The staff should make clear which are the areas, if any, where economies are vulnerable. This assessment should be confidential, but it would be central in monitoring and evaluating the conduct of national macroeconomic policies and the surveillance activities of the IMF. It would be even more important in the context of our proposals for the accountability of an independent IMF, described in Chapter 4.

2.4 Crisis prevention: is pre-qualification the way forward?

2.4.1 Pre-qualification: a sceptical assessment

Many proposals to strengthen crisis prevention include some form of 'pre-qualification' for financial support by the IMF. A minimalist version of this line of thinking (for example, Dornbusch, 1998) is that whenever a country applies for support its previous record should be reviewed: if it ignored warnings in the past, support would be denied. A stricter version is to have a pre-determined list of countries that are eligible for financial support (Calomiris, 1998).

The appeal of conditioning access on a list of prior actions is that it promises to address problems of moral hazard. Governments that turn a deaf ear to Fund calls for remedial action would no longer ignore warnings and follow dangerous policies on the premise that they will be bailed out if their gamble fails. In addition, markets will know which countries are taking risks and would help enforce discipline. But pre-qualification suffers from three flaws:

- First, there is little evidence that government moral hazard is widely present. The record is that following a crisis most governments lose power – not just in democratic countries – and they all know it. The crisis itself is a blow to their claim to economic competence. It often hurts some of the private interests that may have been crucial to their lease on power. And the IMF programmes that follow further erode their power.

- Second, pre-qualification must rest on criteria that will inevitably be arbitrary. The criteria could feature all kinds of variables, including the quality of macroeconomic policy, the strength of the banking system and the direction of reform. But even if the criteria could be agreed relatively easily, what about the threshold? If it were too strict, no country likely to need IMF support would be eligible; if it were too soft, it would be useless. The boundary is difficult to draw, the criteria themselves are not easily amenable to precise quantification, and inevitably, political considerations would interfere. Furthermore, once a country qualified, it would be impossible or politically unfeasible to drop it from the list, especially when that might precipitate a crisis. Over time, most countries would qualify and none would be dropped.

- Third, pre-qualification is not time-consistent: the threat to turn a blind eye to a country that had not pre-qualified is hardly credible. To start with, the IMF always cares about the risk of contagion. After all, fire-fighters do not let a house burn down simply because the occupants lit the fire themselves. In addition, both because of the risk of contagion and for political reasons, big countries would be assisted regardless of how sound their economies, as illustrated by the cases of Brazil, Mexico and Russia.

'Too-big-to-fail' and 'too-geopolitically-important-to-fail' are important arguments that preclude an objective pre-qualification list. Furthermore, while countries like Thailand may not threaten financial stability alone, together with countries like Korea and Malaysia they clearly do. In the end, political considerations will still play a role in the IMF's decisions, and as recent experience has shown, the main shareholders will have considerable influence. If countries with strong ties to the most important shareholders are kept on the list despite weak fundamentals, fairness becomes the concern. So before pre-qualification is seriously considered, the IMF must be made more independent.

2.4.2 Contingent Credit Lines

In April 1999, the IMF's Executive Board agreed 'to provide Contingent Credit Lines (CCL) for member countries with strong economic policies as a precautionary line of defence readily available against future balance of payments problems that might arise from international financial contagion.' By approving access to CCL, countries would be recognized as having strong fundamentals, since participation in this facility is subject to good behaviour conditions (the details are set out in Box 2.6)

The credit lines would be added to the funds that a country is able to obtain through a stand-by arrangement or other facilities. But countries already borrowing under a stand-by programme will not be eligible for the CCL, ruling out countries that exhibit macroeconomic weaknesses and have an adjustment programme in progress. The intent is to prevent contagious speculation hitting countries in a strong position. In particular, by signalling that countries have a powerful line of defence, it is hoped that self-fulfilling crises can be avoided. Thus, if the CCL actually works, the funds would never be drawn down.

The CCL approach is closely related to the principle of pre-qualification and is subject to all the flaws discussed above. In particular, 'dequalification' of a country previously qualified could precipitate a crisis. Once a country is accepted, therefore, it will be extremely unlikely to lose that status. In the end, this could just

Box 2.6 **The CCL facility**

The IMF's Executive Board agreed to provide Contingent Credit Lines (CCL) to member countries in April 1999.[1] The CCL is an addition to the Supplemental Reserve Facility (SRF) established at the end of 1997. Critically, the SRF is intended for use by member countries already experiencing a crisis, while the CCL is intended as a precautionary measure for countries with fundamentally strong policies but at risk, at some time in the future, of contagion from other parts of the world.

The CCL is not subject to access limits, but there is an understanding that commitments should be in the range of 300–500% of a country's quota. The Directors' decision does, however, make provision for larger commitments in exceptional circumstances and smaller ones if required by the Fund's liquidity position.

Directors set down five criteria for determining whether a country qualifies for the CCL. (Qualification will last for a total of one year, after which the same process will presumably have to be repeated):

1 The member's policies are such that it is unlikely to have to make use of Fund resources; in particular, it is not already experiencing difficulties.

2 The outcome of the last Article IV consultation was positive.

3 It is making sufficient progress in the adoption of internationally accepted standards for financial management.

4 It has 'constructive relations' with its creditors and is taking steps to facilitate private sector involvement in the resolution of its difficulties (possibly including the introduction of collective action clauses into its loan contracts).

5 It has adopted (and shared with the Fund) a satisfactory economic and financial programme.

But meeting these conditions for pre-qualification does not entitle a country to draw on its CCL. Rather, when it requests actual use of the CCL resources, the member must pass a special 'activation' review to determine that no backsliding has occurred since it qualified. In addition, CCL resources can be released in tranches, with later tranches subject to the member meeting specific conditions.

continued

---

1. See 'Executive Board Decision: Contingent Credit Lines' (23 April 1999), www.imf.org/externl/np/sec/pr/1999/pr9914/ttm.

Box 2.6 continued

Countries are expected to repay within one to one and a half years of the date of each disbursement. But the Board may extend the repayment period by up to 12 months. During the first year, the member pays a surcharge of 300 basis points above the rate of charge on regular IMF drawings. The surcharge then increases by 50 basis points for every subsequent six months up a ceiling of 500 basis points.

---

become a way to provide larger support packages with little discrimination among countries. With the current system of political control on the IMF's Executive Board, it is difficult to envisage the objectives of the CCL being achieved effectively.

An additional question is whether countries will apply for the CCL. There is no sign of this to date. Application could be seen as a signal that a country needs protection from some unknown weakness. For countries that have survived the contagion effects from the Mexican and Asian crises, this could be a serious hurdle: after having gone unscathed through much turmoil, why should they find it useful to apply for support now? The Fund might wish to build up the CCL as a status symbol of good economic health, but then the dequalification problem grows even deeper.

Finally, the CCL is adding a new facility to a widening range the Fund has implemented in recent years. The proliferation of lending facilities is itself becoming part of the problem. These facilities need to be streamlined to make emergency lending more transparent, simple and effective.

2.5 Structural policies

For some time now, concern has been growing that the Fund's surveillance activities and programme design have moved on to domestic structural and institutional affairs in a way that could be intrusive.[20] A new debate is emerging: should the Fund stick to the monetary, fiscal and exchange rate policies that have historically been the key determinants of the balance of payments? Or should it go further, involving itself in other areas, such as financial system oversight, corporate governance and bankruptcy laws?

The IMF is right in asserting that macroeconomic policies ultimately fail to improve an economy when its microeconomic structure is fundamentally flawed, and that policy commitments will not be implemented when they clash with private interests entrenched in the political leadership. On the other hand, structural reforms are always risky and controversial: they are risky because we know little about their effects on the economy in the short term, either in theory or in practice; they are controversial because they invariably affect property rights and may provoke a backlash. This is especially likely if the IMF gives the impression that it pushes harder when countries are in crisis.

Over the years, the IMF has developed a systematic approach to macroeconomic policies. Applying a well-tested common treatment to all countries has been a source of legitimacy. Much the same is needed for structural reforms but unfortunately, the Fund lacks expertise in these areas. A good starting point is for the Fund to press for standards and to enforce them. These are needed in several areas: auditing and accounting practices, corporate governance, insolvency legislation, as well as regulation of banks and securities markets.

Part of the burden of designing standards could and should be assumed by independent and specialized agencies, taking into account the practices of emerging markets to make them effective and widely accepted. The Fund should then help to supervise compliance with those internationally agreed standards. For example, the BIS has already established a track record in financial regulation and capital movement oversight, but it is currently hampered by its limited membership. Any grand design could include universal membership of the BIS and an extension of its mandate to the regulation of banks, financial institutions and hedge funds, information disclosure and bankruptcy legislation. Eichengreen (1999) envisages a complete set of standards adopted by professional organizations and by the IMF as part of its routine surveillance.

In summary, the IMF is inevitably drawn into structural issues in conjunction with its surveillance activities. Structural deficiencies are now too important in crises to be ignored. Checking only traditional macroeconomic issues may miss fundamental vulnerabilities. But the Fund lacks the expertise and does not need to invest further in this area given the existence of specialized institutions.

2.6 Conclusions

This chapter makes six main points:

- For its routine surveillance and crisis prevention, the Fund relies on an outdated procedure that underestimates the importance of financial markets.

- This has led the Fund to encourage capital account liberalization without taking the necessary precautions to avoid devastating crises. Similarly, the Fund has adopted a benign view of fixed exchange rate regimes, failing to recognize the danger of maintaining pegs for too long.

- The response to recent crises cannot be simply to improve forecasts. Crises are inherently impossible to forecast and the IMF does not enjoy any comparative advantage in this area over rating agencies and other forecasting services.

- The Fund has a role to play in data dissemination and greater transparency, but it is also limited in this domain by the confidentiality needed to build up trust with its member countries.

- Pre-qualification – as recently implemented with the new CCL facility – is appealing but unlikely to work for a variety of reasons: the criteria are inevitably fuzzy, the approach is time-inconsistent, and politics are sure to interfere.

- The Fund is right to observe that there cannot be lasting good macroeconomics with deficient structures. But the Fund lacks the competence and legitimacy to enforce its own conditions, either through surveillance or within programmes. Standards should be designed by existing specialized agencies and enforced by the IMF.

Most of the shortcomings uncovered here share a common feature. In the brave new world of full capital mobility, economies become vulnerable to a bewildering variety of weaknesses extending far beyond the IMF's traditional macroeconomic brief. While it is naturally drawn into widening its role, the Fund often finds itself lacking expertise and authority. Both lead to political difficulties and call for reviewing the Fund's own structure.

With capital mobility, policy analysis and prescription become both more sophisticated and less sure-footed. Not only is the Fund's authority undermined, but conflicts between staff and management, or between different departments within the Fund, arise more frequently.[21] More generally, different departments often produce different and conflicting policy recommendations. Currently, the Fund's management decides on the issue before it is presented to the Executive Board discussion, while the Executive Board can make an informed decision only if it is provided with the opposing viewpoints. Forming a unified position is necessary for such an organization, but the need for accountability grows along with the complexity of the issues.

Similarly, the Fund cannot ignore sensitive issues such as the need to reform banking systems and financial markets, the exchange rate regime, corporate governance, or the quality of information released by member governments. Its authority in these matters needs to be enhanced, but it is bound to infringe on member countries' sovereignty. The only possibility is to recognize that accountability and sovereignty are related: the more accountable the Fund is to its membership, the stronger is its legitimacy in dealing with sensitive issues that may be seen as infringing on sovereignty. Progress on the former is a pre-condition for extending the Fund's mandate on the latter.

More generally, as the Fund's missions become less narrowly technical, the risk of politicization grows. To be sure, the IMF has never been a purely technocratic institution but the risks have been magnified by the combination of two related changes. First, as repeatedly noted above, capital account liberalization requires a wider and deeper mandate, extending well beyond monetary and fiscal policy. Second, the countries in need of IMF programmes are now all in the developing world, a sharp change from the situation at the time of Bretton Woods. Yet a lasting legacy of Bretton Woods is that the Fund's Executive Board is dominated by the developed countries.

A new equilibrium must be found, and it is likely to be based on more operational independence from the large shareholders, which in turn will require more accountability. Chapter 4 makes proposals to improve both independence and accountability.

3 The IMF and Crisis Management

Chapter 2 examined the IMF's procedures in quiet times, when it is not called on to deal with a country's urgent need for support. Chapter 3 focuses on emergencies. It explores how the Fund has responded to the crises of the past years and draws lessons for the future. The first section lays out the challenges that arise during capital account crises. The following section documents and criticizes the trend toward ever-larger IMF loans. The next two sections look at fiscal and monetary policy responses, with particular attention to the nexus linking the exchange rate regime, interest rate defence of the currency, standstills and orderly workouts. The finalsection deals with the politically sensitive issue of structural policy conditions.

3.1 Dealing with capital account crises

Chapter 1 explored how crises have changed in nature. It also argued that in spite of spectacular efforts – much bigger loans, faster disbursements and the introduction of structural conditions – success at dealing with crises has been, at best, limited. In some instances, the Fund has even had to alter its strategy midway. What exactly has gone wrong, and how should the IMF ready itself to face future crises?

At the root of the problem lies the distinction between a liquidity crisis and a crisis related to bad fundamentals – and the need to draw the appropriate policy implications from this distinction. When capital mobility was limited, most crises originated in the current account and resulted from misguided macroeconomic policies. But when capital is highly mobile, crises are different. Liquidity crises arise when foreign loans are suddenly withdrawn and domestic currency assets are liquidated in a frenzy. Just when they need to step in to extinguish budding banking crises and impending bankruptcies, the authorities lose access to foreign financing.

The IMF has gone some way to recognizing the evolving nature of currency crises, but not yet all the way. In the midst of the Asian crisis, for example, the Fund introduced the Supplemental Reserve Facility (SRF), designed to provide large amounts of financial support when urgently required. Following the Asian crisis, it has further set up the Contingent Credit Lines (CCL) facility, discussed – and criticized – in Chapter 2. The SRF may help alleviate a liquidity crisis, but when it was first used in Korea, it did not prevent an economic implosion there.[22] One possible explanation is that it was accompanied by the wrong sort of conditionality.

A fundamentals-based crisis typically calls for general macro-economic policy tightening, precisely the sort of adjustment the IMF routinely requires. But while some weak fundamentals will invariably lie at its root, a liquidity crisis need not be caused by lax macroeconomic policies. It therefore does not systematically require the same policy reaction.

Liquidity crises are temporary in nature. Their resolution calls for temporary support: foreign financing to maintain market access – hence the usefulness of the SRF – and domestic financing to prevent a meltdown or to 'jump-start' the economy by bailing out the banking and financial systems if they have collapsed. Fiscal policy tightening is generally unwarranted though the case of monetary policy is more delicate: a temporary hike in the interest rate may be helpful if it reassures investors.

The solution to a liquidity crisis thus calls for adequate IMF financing and front-loaded disbursement. But should it always be a large package? Where the underlying weaknesses require deep reforms, the Fund should provide limited support – of the order of 100% of a country's quota for a year or 300% of the quota for three years. This should be usually sufficient to avoid an unnecessarily severe recession.

When the country and its creditors conclude that the required adjustment can be undertaken without debt restructuring, co-financing with the private sector – rollovers and rescheduling – is the way forward. When, however, a restructuring of external obligations is unavoidable, the Fund may need to provide larger packages if that is what it takes to 'bail-in' the private sector and prevent costly contagion. The risk is that the private sector sees a big loan as an opportunity to escape and bail out, so any large package must include an explicit agreement with foreign debtors.

3.2 Loan size

3.2.1 Loan size drift

One of the stunning changes since the Mexican crisis has been the growth of IMF lending. Traditionally, loans provided as part of IMF programmes were limited to three times a country's quota. Mexico's loan violated this tradition. The US $50 billion package, of which the IMF contributed US $17.8 billion, amounted to 18 times quota with around US $12 billion (five times quota) actually disbursed.

This arrangement was partly a fig-leaf, partly a necessit, and certainly a precedent. It was a fig-leaf because the entire package was technically an IMF loan: the terms were those of a traditional IMF programme; the agreement was signed with the IMF; and the conditions were set by the IMF alone.[23] It was a necessity because the Fund could not blatantly violate its own rules on the size of the loan as a multiple of a country's quota and because the amount exceeded the IMF's capacity to lend. To assemble packages of this magnitude, the Fund had to act as lead manager, rounding up funds from other sources while still seeking to retain control of the terms.

There was a good reason to adopt a new approach: Mexico was facing a liquidity crisis, mainly operating through the capital account. To be sure, Mexico in 1994 had a large current account deficit, its reserves had been declining, and their imminent exhaustion ultimately left the authorities no choice but to devalue. Following the devaluation, however, the peso continued to decline instead of stabilizing as expected, losing half of its pre-crisis value in a week. The nature of the problem changed: by early January 1995, Mexico was facing massive capital account problems, which dwarfed the earlier current account deficits. Loss of confidence triggered the wholesale liquidation of Mexican assets, including the now infamous dollar-indexed, exchange rate risk-free *tesobonos*.

Capital account crises were not new, of course. But the violence of the event and, above all, the volatility of the capital account were an alarming surprise.

Capital account liberalization has, of course, been underway since the 1980s. As a result, few obstacles now deter investors who wish to invest for the short term and who may withdraw their funds from a country at very short notice. Investors who want to build up large positions can do so at low cost and low risk, especially when the authorities are on the other side of the market – as they inevitably are when seeking to peg the value of their currency. The willingness of the IMF to lend a hand is, in a way, the logical culmination of its having encouraged this earlier financial liberalization. IMF loans, which used to be tailored to current account deficits, now must be calibrated to much larger capital movements.

Table 3.1 **IMF stand-by loans: annual number, total amounts and average sizes** (SDR billions)

	1970	1971	1972	1973	1974	1975	1976
Number	19	16	18	13	13	15	13
Total (SDR bns)	418	487	452	294	1325	1616	690
Average size	22	30	25	23	102	108	53

	1977	1978	1979	1980	1981	1982	1983
Number	19	12	20	22	22	21	30
Total (SDR bns)	4726	1080	1333	3606	5335	2448	6576
Average size	249	90	67	164	243	117	219

	1984	1985	1986	1987	1988	1989	1990
Number	21	25	22	11	15	12	12
Total (SDR bns)	3905	2528	2251	2156	2654	2068	2025
Average size	186	101	102	196	177	172	169

	1991	1992	1993	1994	1995	1996	1997
Number	20	16	13	18	21	13	10
Total (SDR bns)	5873	3463	1643	2601	19085	3534	27022
Average size	294	216	126	145	909	272	2702

Source: International Financial Statistics, various issues.

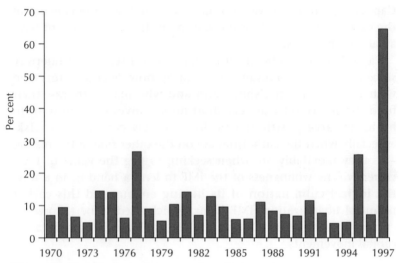

Figure 3.1 Stand-by loans (per cent of world exports)

Source: International Financial Statistics CD-ROM

Table 3.1 shows the number and size of stand-by loans between 1970–97. Despite the increase in IMF membership since 1970, the number of programmes does not exhibit an increasing trend. There was an increase in the mid-1980s, the period of the developing country debt crises, but otherwise stability.[24] At the same time, there has been a steady trend towards larger loans.

Of course, world trade and GDP have grown over the last three decades, so that even if the loans were designed to deal with current account deficits, we would expect to observe a rising trend. Figure 3.1 corrects for this effect in presenting the total annual value of loans as a percentage of total world exports. The figure reveals three extraordinary years: 1977, due to the UK programme; 1995 and 1997, during the Mexican and Asian crises.

In October 1994, shortly before the Mexican crisis, the IMF had decided that stand-by agreements could be as large as 300% of a country's quota. Although this is the amount (US $7.8 billion) that was initially pledged to Mexico out of the Fund's own resources, the total package eventually breached this ceiling by a huge amount. This was partly due to the opposition of the US Congress to a bilateral aid plan of US $40 billion, which forced the IMF to turn to other sources. Some money was provided by the G-10 countries led by the United States. Another US $10 billion expected from high-income non-G-10 countries never materialized, and the Fund ended up committing US $17.8 billion of its own resources. This precedent was used when the IMF designed its package for Thailand. IMF support amounted to 500% of Thailand's quota (US $4 billion). Additional funds were provided through a Japanese initiative, supported by Asian countries, on 11 August 1997 (see Table 3.2).[25] The size of the loan was calibrated to Thailand's debt service needs, including private liabilities, which had been quickly underwritten by the Thai authorities as the crisis began. The same basic procedure was used for the Indonesian crisis that followed, except the bilateral support was in the category of 'second line of defence'.

Again, it seemed prudent to give the arrangement official status. The response took the form of the SRF, adopted just in time to deal with the Korean crisis. Korea received 500% of its quota under a stand-by agreement, and 1500% of its quota under the SRF. The SRF loan came with a one-year programme and a penalty interest rate (much higher than market rate). The Fund's own pledge reached a whopping US $21 billion, nearly 20 times Korea's quota. Ironically, even this was not enough. The total loan package for Korea came to US $57 billion.

Table 3.2 **The recent rescue packages** (in US $ billions)

	Mexico 1 Feb 1995	Thailand 20 Aug 1997	Indonesia 5 Nov 1997	Korea 4 Dec 1997	Brazil Nov 1998
Total of which:	50	17.2	40	57	
IMF	17.8[a]	4	10	21	18
Japan		4.3[b]	3[c]	5[c]	1.25[b]
US		0	5[c]	10[c]	5.0[b,d]
World Bank	20	1.5[b]	4.5[c]	10[c]	4.5[b]
IDB/ADB		1.2[b]	3.5[c]	4[c]	4.5[b]
IMF contribution (% of quota)	500%	500%	500%	2000%	600%

Sources: IDB for Mexico and Brazil, and ADB for Asian countries.

Notes: a of which $12 bilion was actually disbursed.
   b *Pari passu* arrangement.
   c Second line of defence. There were no disbursements from these.
   d Through BIS. For Brazil, through BIS, US contributed 5.0; UK, France, and Germany, 1.25 each; and Canada, Italy, Spain, and Switzerland combined up to 4.5.

The SRF is expressly designed to deal with a 'sudden and disruptive loss of market confidence'. It can be disbursed quickly and is available for one year at a penalty rate. This facility has now been used not only for Korea in 1997, but also for Russia in July 1998 and for Brazil in November 1998. The Korean programme was not an instant success, and a standstill on debt service was subsequently added. In Russia and Brazil, the stated aim was to provide a line of defence for the exchange rate peg. In both cases, the peg soon collapsed under market pressure. Together these three cases demonstrated that even the new larger loan amounts could be insufficient in the face of a capital account crisis.

3.2.2 Small is beautiful?

By encouraging discussion of a possible lender-of-last-resort function and by promoting large CCL facilities, the Fund seems intent on continuing its recent trend of ever-larger loans. Yet the recent experience with drift in loan size suggests three important conclusions that should not be overlooked:

■ It is not always clear that large loans work better than smaller ones, but they clearly aggravate moral hazard problems.
■ If the Fund is to continue to offer loans of a size commensurate with potential capital account imbalances, new financing schemes will be needed.
■ The larger the loans, the more important it becomes that the IMF has a clear governance structure and that it is clearly accountable to its ultimate constituency.

The natural implication is to settle for a 'Goldilocks solution' – loans that are neither too big nor too small – and to make case-by-case decisions. Loans should be sufficient to allow for maintenance of essential debt service, but they should not be so large as to finance a blanket bail-out.

In the case of a liquidity crisis, as in Korea, a large loan could be the right answer, but it would have to be accompanied by high interest rates to help reverse capital flows. If, after a short period, interest rates do not decline and the currency does not stabilize, it is likely that macroeconomic or structural weaknesses are preventing a return of market confidence. Then, the underlying problem – deficits, inflation, banking system fragility, etc. – would have to be addressed directly with the support of a reasonable but not excessive IMF loan. One solution is to announce a package that includes several instalments (the SRF explicitly includes at least two tranches), observe reactions after the announcement and the first disbursement, and suspend further disbursements if the desired results do not materialize.

When large loans are considered – and this should be the exception – it is essential to mitigate the associated moral hazard. To do so, the IMF must involve both sovereign and private debtors. In Korea, G-7 central banks used moral suasion to encourage debtors to roll over their debts, but this was done under unusual conditions that may not be present again in the future. In the absence of private support, the Fund may have to commit to providing only loans of moderate size. By committing not to exceed a given amount (for example, three times a country's quota) the Fund will dispel the expectation that it always stands ready to provide a large bail-out. Debtors will be left with a stark choice: restructure or suffer the consequences of a default.

3.2.3 How to pay for larger loans

Loans of up to five times a country's quota – 20 times quota in the case of the SRF – put extreme pressure on the Fund's resources, which were designed at a time of low capital mobility and limited loan size. Figure 3.2 displays the Fund's liquidity ratio – the ratio of its net uncommitted usable resources to its liquid liabilities. The ratio is now at an all-time low. It was barely recovering from the drain suffered during the debt crisis of the mid-1980s when the Mexican, Asian, Russian and Brazilian maxi-loans were arranged.

When the Fund is in need of additional resources, it must follow a long and haphazard procedure. Traditionally, its resources are entirely made up of contributions by member countries. Any increase in resources must therefore be accepted by the membership in a procedure where large countries, which provide the bulk of the contributions (as remunerated loans rather than grants), have a dominating influence, and where the United States has a veto.

The last procedure for a resource enlargement started in 1998 and lasted for more than the year. It was long tied up in the US Congress, entangled with purely domestic politics, and that delay

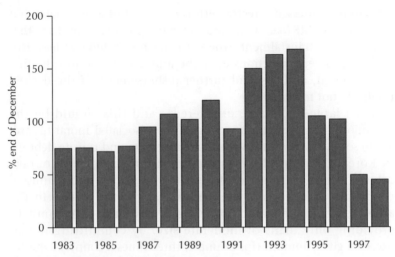

Figure 3.2 The IMF's liquidity ratio (per cent)

Source: IMF

opened the way to renewed debates about the role of the Fund. This is clearly a very inefficient approach.

The obvious solution is to allow the Fund to issue debt under its own signature, much as the World Bank does. This is an old idea, often discussed, if only because it has much merit and does not require a change in the IMF Articles of Agreement. A recent study (Lerrick, 1999) argues that the cost of borrowing from financial markets would be the same as the interest currently paid to member governments. So why is such borrowing not happening?

Opposition comes from several quarters. Staff and others feel that the IMF ought to retain its traditional definition as a fund, pooling and redistributing national resources, a symbol of international cooperation. Others fear that a privately financed IMF would become more sensitive to financial market interests. Yet another argument – to which we largely subscribe – is that easier access to external finance would only encourage loan size drift and 'mission creep'. In the end, true opposition comes from the large share-holders, which understandably fear losing their political influence. Since we argue that the key reform is to free the Fund from politicization, we believe that shifting to market borrowing is a step in the right direction, provided that loan size drift is firmly held in check.

<u>3.3</u> Fiscal policy

Unsustainable current account deficits are typically – though not always – associated with fiscal deficits. This is the so-called Lawson doctrine, which argues that a current account deficit attributable to an excess of private investment over private saving is by definition a sustainable deficit. As a general proposition, the doctrine was discredited by the Mexican and Asian crises, both problems of current account unsustainability not predominantly attributable to fiscal imbalances.

Even in the presence of exchange rate overvaluation, a depreciation restores external balance only when it is accompanied by expenditure-reducing policies (see Dornbusch, 1980). In such a situation, the IMF's insistence on tight monetary and fiscal policies is justifiable and effective. Most of the recent Asian crises occurred with modest current account and budget deficits. Indeed, Korea never had a deficit before or after the crisis. Of recent crises, only in Russia and Brazil has there been a serious fiscal problem. This explains the criticism of the Fund's early insistence that Asian fiscal policies be tightened.

The Fund's own assessment of the Asian crisis (Lane et al., 1999) accepts that fiscal policy was too tight, but it fails to acknowledge fully the impact of this policy. It continues to argue that the depth of the ensuing recession came as a surprise, creating larger fiscal imbalances than expected. It also claims to have reacted promptly once the magnitude of the drop in output became visible. As Table 1.3 indicated, the surprise was massive.

Why was the recession so deep? The IMF's view is that the impact of the twin currency and banking crises was larger than initially expected because the authorities were reluctant to close down banks and take appropriate action to restore confidence. Another view is that the recession was at least partly a consequence of the very policies recommended by the Fund. In this view, the tight fiscal and monetary measures effectively bankrupted banks, finance companies and firms, if only because strict limits on the deficit and on money creation blocked any attempt at rescue. A credit crunch ensued as failed banks were unable to lend and, in any case, would not have granted loans to failed businesses.

This credit crunch explains the depth of the recession. Faced with such an economy-wide banking panic, the usual prescription is a massive injection of cash by the central bank and/or the Treasury designed to restart the credit process and halt the spread of bankruptcies. Having recommended an extra-tight monetary policy to stem the collapse of the exchange rate, the Fund could have advocated emergency intervention by the Treasury and provided the necessary resources. The budget deficit would have had to widen but the plunge in economic and financial activity would have been cushioned.

According to this view, the Fund did not simply make a forecast error; it created the conditions for the error. Why did the Fund opt for tight fiscal policy? Some would say that it instinctively applied its standard operating procedures. Others have suggested that it feared Sargent and Wallace's (1981) 'unpleasant arithmetic'. This warns that unsustainable budget deficits are eventually monetized: when the government can no longer finance its debt through non-inflationary borrowing, the central bank is forced to print money. In this case, the debt build-up that a bank rescue would have caused would have been interpreted as a loss of anti-inflationary credibility, triggering a further meltdown of the exchange rate.

According to this view, the critics' inflationary medicine would have been worse than the disease. The argument is persuasive but misses an essential point: jump-starting the credit mechanism through budget deficits is not an unsustainable fiscal policy because it is a one-off measure, which would in any case largely finance itself by restarting economic growth and thereby generating additional future tax receipts. Fiscally responsible governments may make exceptional interventions like this without losing credibility.

Indeed, one can argue that the IMF's recommended fiscal and monetary policies were unsustainable and harmful to the authorities' credibility precisely because they were bound to result in a credit crunch.[26] The Fund's task, in this view, was to facilitate immediate bank restructuring and help the authorities restart the domestic economy, while at the same time encouraging future fiscal rectitude.

<u>3.4</u> Monetary policy, exchange rate defence, standstills and 'bail-ins'

3.4.1 Can a currency peg be salvaged with high interest rates?

A particularly delicate issue in crisis management concerns monetary policy and how to deal with the exchange rate once the currency comes under attack. In Mexico, the IMF was invited in only after the exchange rate had spiralled downward. Once the programme was adopted, the exchange rate stabilized and partly recovered. In Asia, the Fund was called in earlier, as the exchange rate began to collapse. And in Russia and Brazil, the currency had been under pressure for some time but had not yet given way when the IMF negotiated a programme; in both cases, the currency subsequently fell off its peg (Box 3.1 outlines the Russian story).

The one common feature of all of these cases is that the IMF provided additional funds to augment remaining foreign exchange reserves and advocated raising interest rates to stabilize the currency. Where capital is mobile, this strategy is risky: the case of Sweden in 1992, when the authorities raised marginal lending rates to 500% and still eventually gave up, makes clear exactly how risky.[27] Raising interest rates in the face of an attack will not diffuse market pressures unless the authorities' commitment to those higher rates is credible. When high interest rates inflict pain on the economy, the markets may infer that the authorities cannot hold out much longer. High interest rates carry serious costs – stress in the banking sector as credit demand falls and sharp declines in consumption and investment demand – which must be carefully balanced against the chances of success or a prompt realization that the peg is not defensible.

Another lesson from Europe concerns the use of foreign exchange reserves. Defending a parity through exchange rate interventions aims to change market sentiment by signalling the authorities' willingness to put their money where their mouths are. But if the market remains convinced that a depreciation is unavoidable, speculators may respond by raising the ante and doubling up their positions to make up for what they regard as temporary losses incurred on the way to big gains. If intervention is seen as a sign of desperation, it will only fuel speculative pressure.

Box 3.1 **Why did the Russian rescue fail?**

By mid-1997, Russian interest rates had declined to record low levels of below 20% (see Figure B3.1). With inflation quickly approaching the single-digit range, real interest rates were still high but finally on the same scale as those in other transition countries. Macroeconomic conditions were becoming 'normal'. But then things started to go wrong. By December 1997, with inflation declining further, interest rates reached 35%, and 65% in June 1998. In mid-July, the IMF pledged another US $10 billion, and quickly disbursed half of that amount. Less than a month later, having spent more than US $4 billion on the foreign exchange market, the Russian central bank had to abandon the rouble, which lost half its value in a week, and went on depreciating to stand at about a quarter of its July 1998 value.

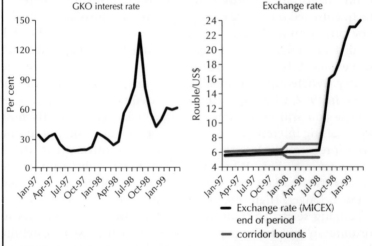

Figure B3.1 Interest rates and exchange rates in Russia
Source: Russian-European Centre for Economic Policy

What went wrong? The story is simple, a textbook case of what not to do. The markets were obviously betting on an exit of the rouble from its 15%-wide corridor. In the face of dwindling tax receipts, the only widely traded Russian asset – the public debt – was increasingly viewed as default grade. This was not because of a temporary shortfall in tax revenues but the symptom of a generalized loss of payment discipline, which included the build-up of pervasive

continued

Box 3.2 continued

payment arrears. A corrupt and highly inefficient tax service was letting profit-reporting firms evade tax payments. At the same time, the highest authorities were unable or unwilling to prosecute tax evaders, in particular the largest corporations, instead offering tax amnesties at regular intervals. The conditions attached by the IMF to its latest loans were all the right ones. But they were detached from economic reality.

The public debt – mostly short-term bills (GKOs) – was held by three groups of investors: the state-owned savings bank, Sberbank; private Russian banks and firms; and foreigners. The foreigners seemed to believe in indefinite IMF bail-outs. Private Russian bankers were rushing for the exit, downloading GKOs and using the proceeds to buy dollars and invest abroad. Their counterparties were: Sberbank, which was officially trying to defend the value of GKOs, but in fact bailing out the bankers; and the central bank, which was providing the dollars out of reserves that were drying up. By the end of June, there were no buyers of GKOs or roubles, hence the idea of applying for a new IMF loan. As soon as the loan reached Moscow, capital flight resumed in an endgame frenzy.

When markets can mobilize sums that vastly exceed the reserves of most authorities, external support in the form of limited IMF loans is unlikely to be a credible deterrent.

3.4.2 Standstills

When public and private debts are large and mostly denominated in foreign currency, maintaining an exchange rate peg is not merely an attempt to fight inflation or preserve the monetary authorities' credibility. It also affects the ability to service debt. The repeated experience is that when an exchange rate depreciates in the midst of a crisis, it becomes massively undervalued. Over time, the undervaluation is gradually erased through a nominal appreciation, higher inflation or a combination of both. (Figure 3.3 illustrates this pattern, showing the real exchange rate of the Mexican peso against the US dollar.)[28]

The impact of such swings on debt service is considerable. For example, if the foreign currency debt amounts to 40% of GDP,

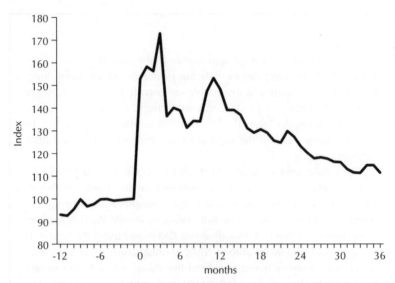

Figure 3.3 The real exchange rate around crisis time (Bilateral real exchange rate of Mexico against US dollar)
Index = 100 on the month before crisis.

Source: International Financial Statistics.

each 10% depreciation increases the debt to GDP ratio by 4%. In these circumstances, a deep devaluation inevitably bankrupts private borrowers and forces government to default. And aiming for low interest rates to revive the economy can turn out to be counterproductive.

One way to evade this unpalatable choice is to suspend debt service until the real exchange rate has recovered and debt service is back to pre-crisis levels, which may take two or three years. Here again, however, the consequences may be devastating. The Mexican moratorium of 1982 made a lasting impression. It triggered a rolling crisis that turned the 1980s into the 'lost decade' for Latin America. For seven long years, Latin America was shut out of international capital markets. Since then, policy-makers have understandably taken a negative view of standstills.

The case against standstills is strong. Moral hazard looms large, and countries should not regard them as normal practice. On the other side, like firms and individuals, countries may be temporarily illiquid and unable to honour their commitments. When the choice is between an interest rate defence of the currency, which can lead to a credit crunch, bank failures and a wave of bankrupt-cies, and a deep devaluation with similar consequences, hitherto unorthodox solutions should not necessarily be ruled out. The appeal of standstills is even stronger if they are conducted in an organized way, allowing for orderly debt rescheduling and a continuation of market access, in contrast to the Latin American experience in the lost decade.

In fact, the IMF has already begun to acknowledge the validity of these arguments and is cautiously adapting its policies accordingly. In 1997, the IMF initially addressed the Korean crisis by providing a large loan, anticipating that ample finance and concerted adjustment would be enough to beat back the attack on the won. When, within a month, it became clear that the loan was not working and that Korea was on the brink of a moratorium, the IMF moved forcefully to avoid a default. It enlisted G-7 support to exert moral suasion on banks: maturing debts were voluntarily rolled over and maturing bank loans were then converted into long-term bonds.

More recently, the Fund has made debt restructuring by Ukraine a prerequisite for the extension of financial support by setting targets for international reserves incompatible with the mainten-ance of full interest payments and principal repayments. It has also supported Paris Club efforts to demand comparable treatment of bondholders as a prerequisite for restructuring Pakistan's official debts (see Box 3.2 below).

3.4.3 Creating viable alternatives to ever-bigger bail-outs

Although the Korean example may be hard to replicate, it shows the possibility of using standstills and 'bailing in' the private sector. The IMF cannot continue to provide ever-bigger loans to finance ever-bigger capital account imbalances. Not only are its resources inadequate, but steadily escalating loan sizes create unsustainable moral hazard problems.

Instead, the Fund must develop an alternative to throwing money at the problem. Those who believe that the market should be allowed to take the lead urge the Fund to stand back and allow nature to run its course. A crisis country should be encouraged to suspend payments and restructure its debts, they argue. The suspension and restructuring would mean that its foreign creditors do not escape without consequence. Meanwhile, a loan limited to three times quota would allow essential trade credits to be maintained and avoid gratuitously disrupting the country's international business.

This approach is in fashion: US Treasury Secretary Rubin's 21 April 1999 speech on reforming the international financial architecture emphasized the need to contain moral hazard and force private creditors to take a hit. Unfortunately, this may be a classic example of a time-inconsistent policy: however appealing the notion that the Fund should limit its assistance *ex ante*, since defaults are messy, expensive and disruptive, there is an inevitable temptation to provide just enough finance to permit suspensions of debt service to be avoided *ex post*.

A credible commitment not to come automatically to the rescue of a country that would otherwise find it impossible to keep current on its obligations, pre-supposes the existence of a mechanism for restructuring outstanding debts. The problem with existing arrangements is that they make work-outs excessively difficult. Since many international bonds include provisions requiring the unanimous consent of bondholders to the terms of a restructuring agreement, there is an incentive for 'vultures' to buy up the outstanding debt and hold the process hostage by threatening legal action. Unlike syndicated bank loans, most bonds lack sharing clauses requiring individual creditors to share with other bondholders any amounts recovered from the borrower. This discourages recourse to lawsuits.

Those who believe that countries may have to take occasional recourse to suspensions and subsequent restructuring therefore argue that these provisions in bond covenants should be modified. Majority voting and sharing clauses would discourage maverick investors from resorting to lawsuits and other ways of obstructing settlements beneficial to the debtor and the majority of creditors alike. Collective representation clauses, which specify who speaks for the bondholders and make provision for a bondholders committee or meeting, would allow orderly decisions to be reached.[29]

This was suggested in 1996 by the G-10 in its post-Mexico report and echoed in a series of recent G-22 and G-7 reports and declarations. In February 1999, the G-7 placed the issue on its work programme for reforming the international financial system with the goal of reaching a consensus by the Cologne summit in June 1999. But nothing was finalized at that summit: the declaration of G-7 finance ministers said that countries should continue to consider including such provisions in their loan agreements, but no concrete steps were recommended to facilitate that process.

If provisions like this are such a good idea, why have the markets not implemented them already? One answer is that neither lenders nor creditors wish to weaken the bonding role of debt by altering loan agreements in ways that might tempt borrowers to walk away from their obligations. Making it easier for debtors to restructure might cause investors to fear that the debtor was prepared to do so at the first sign of trouble, prompting them to liquidate their holdings of its securities. This would precipitate precisely the kind of bond market crisis that the international policy community is concerned to avoid.

But if the bonding role of debt is so fundamental, we would also abolish domestic bankruptcy procedures and reinstate the debtor's prison to prevent domestic borrowers from ever defaulting on their obligations. In fact, in the domestic context, we balance the temptation for debtors to walk away from their obligations against the efficiency advantages, for debtor and creditor alike, of clearing away non-viable debt overhangs and restoring the financial health of fundamentally viable enterprises.

The argument for collective action clauses in bond covenants is an argument for establishing a similar balance in the international bond market. Majority voting, sharing and non-acceleration may make it easier to renegotiate defaulted debts but if this permits a long deadlock to be avoided there will be no reason for investors to shun bonds with these features (see Box 3.2).

A better explanation for why the market has not solved the problem is adverse selection. It is an intrinsic feature of the capital market that lenders know less than borrowers about the latter's willingness and ability to pay. Hence, for the same reason that only patients who anticipate succumbing to a fatal disease will buy expensive life insurance, only countries that anticipate a high probability of having to restructure their debt may wish to issue securities with these provisions. Left to its own devices, neither market may function. The danger is that adverse selection would render the market in these modified bonds illiquid and thereby impair the ability of developing countries to borrow.

Box 3.2 **Recent efforts to 'bail in' the private sector: Ukraine and Pakistan**

Two recent attempts to deal with the problem of private sector burden sharing are Ukraine and Pakistan. Ukraine came to the IMF in the wake of Russia's default, which preceded by a month the maturity date for a tranche of its domestic treasury bills. The country's fear was that its creditors would refuse to roll over these maturing debts in the volatile global financial climate that followed the Russian crisis.

The IMF's worry, in turn, was that any loan would simply go to pay off the holders of these maturing bills. The Fund therefore made its loan conditional on a target for Ukrainian foreign exchange reserves that prevented the authorities from using it to pay off the country's maturing debts. Faced with this constraint, Ukraine was able to induce many of its creditors to exchange their maturing treasury bills voluntarily for zero-coupon eurobonds. Those who resisted were paid in domestic currency, which could not be repatriated.

This restructuring worked relatively smoothly: in particular, Ukraine did not suffer the lawsuits of which many observers warned. The reason was that the bonds in question were governed by Ukrainian law, which made legal recourse unattractive. But it also means that Ukraine's case is unlikely to be a good guide for the future, where the problem will be to restructure eurobonds subject to UK or Luxembourg law.

This possibility was contemplated recently in the case of Pakistan, when the Paris Club, as a condition of extending the country's debt relief on its official credits, required the country to seek comparable treatment from eurobond holders. Here the threat of lawsuits was real, and largely in response, the government found ways, for the time being at least, of averting default on its eurobond debt. In other words, private creditors were not bailed in.

The contrast between the two cases points up the need to introduce sharing, majority voting and collective representation clauses into eurobond covenants that are subject to legal recourse in the courts of countries other than that of the issuer.

The G-10's 1996 report, where the idea of collective action clauses was first mooted, says little about this dilemma. While acknowledging the first-mover problem and suggesting that official support for contractual innovation should be provided 'as appropriate', it failed to specify concrete steps to be taken by the authorities. The G-22 and G-7 also acknowledged the problem, but again failed to commit to specific action. The G-22 recommended that unnamed governments, presumably those of the United Kingdom and the United States, should 'examine' the use of such clauses in their own sovereign bond issues. The G-7 recommended that its members should 'consider' them.

Secretary Rubin, in his April 1999 speech, reiterated that the international community should 'encourage' their broader use. But the official community needs to do more than examine, consider and encourage. Given the adverse selection problem, progress is unlikely without the introduction of actual legislation and regulations in the creditor countries. And without progress on this front, the international community will lack credibility when it insists that it will not automatically come to the rescue of crisis-stricken countries.

The way forward would be for the IMF to urge its member countries to make it a condition for admission to domestic markets that international bond provisions include majority representation, sharing, non-acceleration, minimum legal action threshold and collective representation clauses, where these last provisions allow an indenture trustee to represent and coordinate the bondholders. The Fund should provide an incentive for countries to do so by indicating that it is prepared to lend at more attractive interest rates to countries that issue debt securities featuring these provisions.[30]

3.5 Structural conditions

Chapter 2 documented the IMF's extension of surveillance to structural areas and noted that there are good reasons to go beyond traditional fiscal and monetary policy. With this conclusion in mind, this section asks whether the right time to introduce much needed structural reforms is in the aftermath of a crisis.

3.5.1 The example of bank closures in Asia

Liquidity crises do not occur randomly: there must be some pre-existing structural weakness. As in Latin America in the 1980s, the

Asian and Russian crises have highlighted the fragility of banking in emerging markets. The roots of this weakness are familiar: insufficient diversification, excessive loans to government-sponsored borrowers, poor bookkeeping, unwillingness to acknowledge non-performing loans, sketchy regulation and inadequate supervision. Among the consequences are unhedged foreign currency borrowings, which cannot be serviced when the exchange rate moves by an unexpectedly large amount, leaving an enormous number of non-performing loans. Does all this mean that the IMF should try to impose structural measures in response to liquidity crises, much as it requires macroeconomic adjustments in response to fundamentals-based crises?

Structural measures are usually perceived as more intrusive than macroeconomic policies. Not only does this raise sensitive issues of sovereignty, but emergency structural reforms may be impossible, especially under external pressure. This is illustrated by comparing the cases of Indonesia, Malaysia and Thailand.

In Indonesia, after a few weeks of intense negotiation with the IMF, the authorities agreed on 31 October 1997 to close 16 banks with limited deposit guarantees, one of which belonged to President Suharto's son. In contrast, Thailand had guaranteed all private deposits when suspending 16 finance companies at the end of June 1997. By the time the IMF arrived in Bangkok, another 42 finance companies had been closed. But given the government guarantee, the deposits remained in the banking system.

From the viewpoint of preventing moral hazard, the Indonesian solution was superior, but it caused a bank run and capital flight, which contributed to the sharp decline in the rupiah. In retrospect, it was wise for Thailand to guarantee deposits to prevent a bank run and capital flight while leaving the moral hazard problem for another day.

Malaysia went one step further, protecting banks by propping up real estate and stock prices. Whether this strategy works remains to be seen. Figure 3.4 displays the ratio of bank credit to GDP. The ratio remained roughly unchanged in Indonesia, which means that the stock of credit declined along with GDP. In Malaysia, the ratio increased, which suggests that bank credit at least partially cushioned the fall in output.

Dealing with failed banks is a complicated problem. It is sometimes argued that badly managed banks ought to be closed promptly because forbearance only encourages rent-seeking and

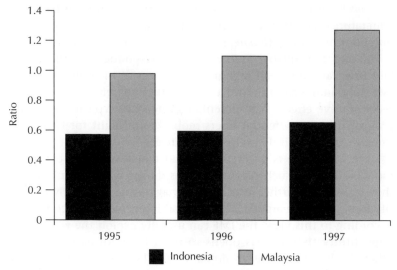

Figure 3.4 The ratio of bank credit to GDP in Indonesia and Malaysia

Source: *International Financial Statistics CR-ROM.*

moral hazard. On closer scrutiny, however, the conclusion is less clear-cut. For a run to be avoided, depositors must be protected and reassured. Furthermore, credit is a factor of production. Its collapse can disrupt trade, both domestically and internationally, doing further damage to banks' balance sheets. These externalities have long been seen as justifying public intervention in response to bank runs and banking panics. Although bad banks should eventually be closed or restructured, this should not always be done at the height of the crisis. Waiting until the panic has passed may be prudent.

3.5.2 The risks with structural policies

For some time, the IMF had been concerned with microeconomic issues, yet it has only recently expanded the range of conditions attached to its programmes. By venturing into this uncharted territory, the IMF exposes itself to new controversies and risks. The Fund's traditional interventions are based on an established body of theoretical and empirical knowledge, some of which has been adduced by IMF staff themselves. In contrast, the microeconomic and sociological base on which the Fund must rely to shape its new conditionality is less advanced. For example, the request that the *chaebols* be dismantled as part of the Korean programme is based on a literature on corporate governance that raises a host of fascinating questions but which, to date, provides few definitive answers.

The fact that microeconomic reforms are politically difficult can be turned around as an argument in favour of including them in IMF programme conditions. Desirable structural reforms often have redistributive effects. The potential gainers are typically a diffuse group while the potential losers mobilize and fight for their self-interest. Here, the IMF can tip the balance.

Moreover, there is an argument that concessions are extracted more easily from such pressure groups during a crisis. Only when they realise that further resistance may aggravate an already serious situation, it can be argued, are potential losers willing to concede.[31] According to this view, the IMF can usefully exploit the window of opportunity that a crisis opens to push for reforms that would otherwise be impossible. In doing so, the IMF acts as an agent of goodwill while accepting the role of scapegoat. A counter-argument is that governments facing a crisis are strained, both in terms of human resources and political capital. A crisis is not the right time to push through reforms that are economically complex and politically contentious. Instead, this is the time to seek unity in facing the immediate challenges.

A key Fund concern in its recent programmes has been to rebuild national authorities' credibility (see Lane et al., 1999). This objective was repeatedly invoked to justify restrictive monetary and fiscal policies. The objective of credibility-building also lies behind structural proposals, such as granting independence to the central bank and changing the fiscal procedures. These measures may be unambiguously welfare-improving, but they are politically contentious when powerful interests benefit from the *status quo*. Yet when structural reforms are too tough (as they were in the 15 January 1998 agreement with Indonesia), the market simply will not believe that they can stick and confidence is lost rather than gained.

Credibility is not established overnight but IMF programmes are negotiated in emergencies and must produce quick results. This tension shows up in two risks:

■ The danger of overemphasizing long-term policies that do not help to bring the immediate crisis to an end. This was the case in Korea, when the IMF requested quick restructuring of the *chaebols*; in Russia, when it asked for improved tax collection; and in Brazil, when it sought to reign in local spending. At the same time as these proposals, in all three cases, the Fund left the exchange rate regime untouched.

■ The risk that including both short-term macroeconomic conditions and deep structural reforms in programmes produces all-encompassing lists, with which governments cannot cope in a crisis. Inevitably, the authorities will sort out what can be done quickly and what can be postponed. The consequence is that conditionality will again be violated, and the Fund will lose credibility.

3.5.3 Guidelines for structural policies

In the final analysis, structural and microeconomic issues are too important for financial stability for the IMF to ignore them. In a world of increasingly integrated capital markets, the international financial system cannot be strengthened without strengthening the domestic financial systems that are its constituent parts. But the IMF should bear in mind three guidelines when contemplating interventions to strengthen the operation of domestic institutions, markets and regulations:

■ First, since the Fund's core responsibility (more now than in the past and presumably even more so in the future) is to foster financial stability, it should focus on structural reforms with a direct impact on the financial sector. At the same time, it should tread cautiously when tempted to trespass into other areas, such as competition policy. It may be difficult to draw a line between structural reforms that are integral to the restoration of *financial* stability and reforms that, while they may be desirable on other grounds, are not essential to this core function. But the Fund needs to make a harder effort to draw this line.

■ Second, not all reforms that will eventually deliver a more robust and durable financial system should be pushed through at the height of a crisis. For example, regulatory forbearance that allows insolvent banks to remain in business indefinitely is bad policy since it allows 'gambling for redemption' of a sort that causes social losses to mount. But closing bad banks at the height of a crisis is an invitation to panic, which, by disrupting the flow of trade credit at the worst possible time, threatens to aggravate recessions unnecessarily. Some initiatives, however necessary in the long run, are best left for another day.

■ Third, the Fund can avoid the accusation that its structural interventions are arbitrary, capricious and insensitive to the domestic context if it predicates them on international standards expressly agreed by the international community. For example, it should ground its advice on reform of auditing and accounting practices on the standards promulgated by bodies like the Emerging Markets Subcommittee of the International Accounting Standards Committee. And it should ground its advice on the reform of bankruptcy laws on the standards promulgated by the International Bar Association. Only then will the Fund be protected from the criticism that it is imposing arbitrary structural conditions in whose formulation the emerging markets themselves have had no say.

3.6 Conclusions

When crisis prevention fails, as inevitably happens on occasions, the IMF finds itself facing many challenging tasks. Capital mobility strongly sharpens policy choices and makes it indispensable to diagnose the situation correctly. Standard 'off-the-shelf' macro-economic recipes are no longer enough, nor are they necessarily appropriate in the presence of liquidity crises triggered by microeconomic weaknesses.

The Fund needs to move in a number of directions:

■ Financial programming based on the time-honoured Polak model, designed to deal with current account and fiscal imbalances, tends not to focus on what matters: capital flows and market expectations. Its simplicity, long a key advantage, is now turning into a serious liability.

■ The trend toward ever-larger loans is a natural response to ever-larger capital flows, but it may be an endless pursuit. The record so far is not so good. Under particular circumstances, pure liquidity crises may be dealt with by large loans. But in general, smaller loans are desirable: they can be efficient if properly supported by other measures and they reduce the scope for moral hazard.

- Defending an exchange rate peg has proven to be nearly impossible in the face of a deep loss of market confidence. The defence itself is expensive (huge loans, dangerously high interest rates and credit crunches), it provides markets with perverse incentives (speculation and offshore borrowing) and, when it fails, it results in dramatic economic and political collapses. A preferable strategy involves cutting the losses early, allowing exchange rate flexibility and recognizing that in some instances fiscal policy measures may be useful in jump-starting the economy while extreme fiscal tightening will make the recession worse.

- When crises are triggered by microeconomic weaknesses, it seems reasonable to include structural policies as a part of conditionality. But since structural policies are often interfering with sovereignty, they must be used parsimoniously and only if the chance of success is high. Working against them is limited knowledge and the fact that they usually produce their effects with considerable delay – well beyond the horizon of a crisis – and they can be easily evaded.

- This does not mean that the IMF should ignore structural policies altogether. It should encourage and monitor the adoption of standards developed by specialized institutions.

- The exchange rate undervaluation that characterizes most crises makes debt service nearly impossible. Preserving the integrity of loan contracts is a key responsibility of the Fund and of the international community but this does not mean that there can be no exceptions. It is possible to organize standstills and debt workouts without creating too severe moral hazard.

Structural policies, standstills and bailing in the private sector all mean that the IMF is wading into new and politically sensitive territory. In these circumstances, the Fund needs to build up both technical and political credibility. The former can be achieved by adopting standards. The latter requires a change in the Fund's governance structure to reduce the risk of political capture.

4 Reforming the IMF

The IMF has come under fire not only for its decisions but also for how it takes them. One criticism is that decision-making in the Fund is dominated by management and staff, who set the agenda for Executive Board discussions and act as the conduit for information flows between crisis countries and the Board. According to this view, the Executive Directors are unable to challenge the recommendations of management and staff or to take control of decision-making.[32] For example, it is said that in 1997–8, staff and management pressed the recommendations of an archaic financial programming model on a Board denied independent perspectives on the Asian crisis.

Another criticism is that the priorities of the IMF's management, staff and principal shareholders differ from those of society as a whole – that the Fund attaches too much weight to monetary and price stability, and inadequate weight to economic growth and an equitable income distribution. In this view, the Fund is too inclined to insist on harsh policies of austerity on detecting the first whiff of inflation, and insufficiently concerned to see the adoption of measures designed to boost economic growth.

A third criticism is that certain national governments – and the United States in particular – exercise a disproportionate influence over the decisions taken by the Fund. In this view, the Fund too often pursues policies that serve the interests of Wall Street and the US State Department rather than the world as a whole. More generally, the critics allege that the Fund is too responsive to its principal shareholders, which are high-income, international creditor countries, the interests of which do not necessarily coincide with those of global society.

These criticisms, while not independent, are distinct. The appropriate responses are distinct as well. If one believes that the problem is to empower the Board by attenuating the information asymmetries on which the agenda-setting power of staff and management rests, then the solution is measures to create new channels for the flow of information within the institution and between the institution and the outside world.

If, on the other hand, the problem is that Directors, management and staff have idiosyncratic objectives that conflict with the institution's social responsibilities, then the solution is to enhance the transparency of IMF operations and the institution's accountability for its actions.

We see some merit in both of these views and suggest some modest reforms to be adopted in response. But if one also believes, as we do, that the fundamental problem is that the IMF is too responsive to the agendas of national governments (the governments of its principal shareholders in particular), then measures to enhance transparency and accountability may not be enough. Giving more power to the Board may then compound the problem of excessive politicization rather than diminishing it. Executive Directors, after all, are answerable to the governments they represent, governments that seek to advance political agendas of their own. In this case, it will be necessary to undertake a far-reaching reform to make the Board independent of governments. That is what we describe below.

<u>4.1</u> The context of IMF decision-making

4.1.1 Voting rules

IMF policy is set by an Executive Board of 24 members accountable to their national governments. While some countries have their own Executive Directors (China, France, Germany, Japan, Russia, Saudi Arabia, the United Kingdom and the United States), other Directors represent groups or 'constituencies' of countries.[33]

Board decisions may be taken by a majority or 'supermajority' vote of Directors depending on the issue, as specified by the Fund's Articles of Agreement (see Box 4.1). Directors' votes are proportional to the quotas of the countries they represent, where quotas are a function of countries' weight in the international economic and financial system. In practice, political inertia – in particular, resistance by incumbents – prevents these weights from being rapidly revised to reflect changes in the importance of different countries to the world economy. The voting power of the United States amounts to 17.56% of the total number of votes, effectively giving the country a veto power on all decisions that require the 85% majority (see Chapter 1 for a detailed analysis of voting shares).

It can be argued that these formalities are less important than it appears, since most Executive Board decisions are taken by consensus and formal dissents are rare. But the Fund only releases summaries of Board discussions, which reveal little information about the substance of disagreements within the Board. The decision-making process is difficult to assess because it is cloaked in secrecy.

Meanwhile, with the liberalization of financial markets and the development of new information and communications technologies, the pace of events in financial markets has been ratcheted up. The Board has been forced to take decisions under growing pressure of time, shifting the balance of power towards staff and management. Staff and management have always played an important role in shaping decision-making by the Board by framing the issues,

Box 4.1 **Decision rules in the Executive Board of the IMF**

General Principle ('Principles')

According to Article XII.3, the Executive Board is responsible for conducting the business of the Fund and exercising all the powers delegated to it by the Board of Governors. Any valid decision by the Executive Board requires a quorum: a majority of Directors representing at least 50% of the total voting power. The Managing Director has no vote except in case of an equal division of votes. According to Article XII.5.c, decisions are taken by majority except when otherwise specified.

Special Majorities ('Majorities')

There are two cases: the 70% majority and the 85% majority.

The 70% majority mainly concerns the following:

Prescriptions of medium of payment for an increase in the quota (Art. III.3.a and d).

Adoption of rules concerning the repurchase by a member country of Fund's holdings in that country's currency (Art. V.7.e).

continued

Box 4.1 continued

Postponement of the repurchase obligations (Art. V.7.g).

Determination of the charges levied by the Fund on a series of operations (Art. V.8.a, b and d).

Imposition of charges in case of a failure to repurchase (Art. V.8.c and d).

Changes in the share of quota granting a remuneration (Art. V.9.c).

Determination of remuneration rates (Art. V.9.a).

Decision to publish a report on member's monetary conditions and developments when the situation of that member causes serious problems to the balance of payments of other members (Art. XII.8).

A series of accounting decisions such as, for example, the distribution from general reserves (Art. XII.6.d), the transfer of currencies in General Resource Account to the Investment Account (Art. XII.6.f.ii) or the method used for the valuation of SDR (Art. XV.2).

Prescription of SDR operations between participants (Art. XIX.2.c).

Adoption, modification or abrogation of rules concerning the reconstitution of SDR used by a member (Art. XIX.6.b).

Determination of rates of interest and charges on SDR (Art. XX.3).

Suspension of voting rights and the termination of that suspension (Art. XXVI.2.b).

The 85% majority mainly concerns:

Changes in quotas (Art. III.2.c).

Prescription of other holders of SDR (non-members, institutions that perform central bank functions for more than one holder) (Art. XVII.3.i).

Allocation and cancellation of SDR (Art. XVIII.2.a, b and c, XVIII.4.a and d).

Provisions for general exchange rate arrangements (Art. IV.2.c).

Changes in periods for repurchase (Art. V.7.c and d).

Various accounting rules.

Adjustment of votes, waiver of conditions and ineligibility to use Fund's general resources (Art. XII.5.b).

Amendment of the Agreement (Art. XXVIII.a).

highlighting what they regard as the key data and laying out feasible policy options. But while the agenda-setting power of staff and management has always influenced IMF decision-making, growing pressure of time has limited the Board's ability to demand staff reports in advance, to analyse the issues independently and to consult with their governments. This has worked to enhance further the ability of staff and management to shape discussions within the Board.

4.1.2 The weight of the United States

One exception to the generalization that influence within the Board has shifted away from national governments in favour of the IMF's permanent employees is the United States. The US government's prominence in international financial markets and large voting share in the Board enable it to exercise a disproportionate influence over decision-making in the Fund.

In particular, the US has effective veto power on all key decisions affecting the structure and rules of the Fund since these decisions typically require the supermajority of 85%. And because the United States is home to the world's leading financial market, unenthu-siastic endorsement of an IMF decision by the US Treasury could doom any IMF agreement that requires participation by the financial markets.

In addition, the US Treasury has the advantage of physical and intellectual proximity to the Fund. From the US government's point of view, it helps that the IMF headquarters is not only in the same time zone but also a two-minute cab ride from the Treasury. That senior economic officials in the US government and senior staff and management of the Fund are products of the same institutions of higher learning means that they speak the same professional language and reason with the same kinds of analytical tools.

4.1.3 Distinct problems require distinct solutions

There are three distinct critiques of decision-making in the Fund:

■ that decisions are pre-empted by management and staff, who have considerable agenda-setting power as a result of information asymmetries;
■ that the Executive Board, staff and management pursue idiosyncratic objectives at the expense of the public interest;

■ and that IMF decision-making is disproportionately influenced by national objectives, particularly those of the US government.

As distinct problems, these critiques call for distinct solutions:

■ Measures to facilitate the flow of information within the institution and between the institution and the outside world are the obvious way of addressing the first problem of information asymmetries.

■ Measures to enhance transparency and accountability are the obvious way of ensuring that Executive Directors pursue their announced goals and making it more costly for them to pursue idiosyncratic objectives.

■ But if the problem is not that governments and Directors have hidden agendas, but rather that they pursue overt national agendas inconsistent with the global interest, then more far-reaching reforms are called for to 'depoliticize' IMF decision-making.

Our proposed solution is an independent Executive Board made up of Directors appointed to long terms in office, prohibited from taking instructions directly from their governments, and account-able to the Interim Committee. We describe this proposal for IMF reform at the end of this chapter.

4.2 Facilitating information flows to empower the Executive Board

If obstacles to the flow of information within the IMF and between the Fund and the outside world vest excessive agenda-setting power in management and staff and limit the decision-making power of the Board, then the solution is to create mechanisms for increasing the flow of information and analysis. This can be done by giving a prospective programme country a seat at the Board table, from where it can directly offer the Board an independent assessment of economic conditions and appropriate solutions, as proposed by Miyazawa (1999).

Currently, government officials visit the Fund to discuss the economic situation with staff and address the Board through their Executive Director. This procedure is strained by the large constituencies served by most Executive Directors of developing countries. Allowing national officials to make their case in the Board would improve the flow of information to the relevant IMF decision-makers.

Information flows could also be improved if the Board convened regular meetings of a panel of academic consultants to offer independent analyses of pressing policy issues, akin to a procedure already followed by the Federal Reserve Board. It would also be helpful to commission regular outside reviews of past IMF programmes, something the Fund already does on an *ad hoc* basis, but which in the future should be done as a matter of course.

While these are useful steps, they would not guarantee that the Board had access to all the same information obtained by management and staff through Article IV consultations and programme-related missions. Inevitably, management would retain some agenda-setting power over the decisions taken by the IMF's shareholders, just as the management of a corporation has some agenda-setting power over the decisions taken by its shareholders.

This kind of 'principal-agent slack' is unavoidable in a large bureaucracy. It is the price of effective management and has two central roles: first, it allows spot decisions when events unfold too quickly for effective decisions to be taken in a shareholder meeting of the whole organization; and second, it filters information when the volume of data would be overwhelming to shareholders whose attention is divided between other matters. But following the analogy with principal-agent problems within the corporation, steps to empower shareholders and limit principal-agent slack by reducing information asymmetries would enhance efficiency. The modest steps described in this section all work in this direction and should be included in any reform of the IMF.

4.3 Enhancing transparency and accountability to achieve better alignment of private and social interests

4.3.1 The case for transparency and accountability

If concern about IMF decision-making is focused on the tendency for Executive Directors, staff and management to pursue private agendas, then the solution is to enhance transparency and accountability. Take three possible scenarios:

■ that there is agreement that the task for Executive Directors is to advance policies that promise to maintain and restore domestic and international financial stability, but that some Directors instead pursue idiosyncratic goals;

■ that some countries pre-occupied by security considerations are anxious to prop up the centrist government of a country where an extremist takeover would have undesirable geopolitical repercussions;

■ or that Directors, staff and management attach excessive weight to price and exchange rate stability relative to the importance society attaches to measures designed to stimulate economic growth.

In all these cases, greater transparency of decision-making would work to reveal these hidden agendas and therefore have the socially desirable effect of strengthening the Fund's incentives to pursue socially desirable goals.

In addition, because greater transparency will better enable the Fund to develop a reputation for valuing policy measures that strengthen stability, private sector expectations will be rendered more sensitive and responsive to Fund policies. Greater transparency will also deepen public understanding of IMF conditionality, in turn enhancing the stabilizing effect of its recommendations. Capital flight should then become less of a problem, and arranging private sector co-financing of IMF programmes will become easier.

Thus, quite independently of reputational considerations, greater transparency would strengthen the catalytic role of the Fund. But while society should prefer more transparency to less, an IMF run by shareholders with idiosyncratic agendas will tend to prefer less transparency to more since less transparency means more discretion to pursue idiosyncratic goals at less cost to the reputation of the institution.[34]

4.3.2 Against consensus decision-making

The obvious way to enhance IMF accountability is by requiring more decisions to be taken by formal up-or-down votes and releasing the results. Directors' ultimate constituencies will then be in a position to judge whether or not their representatives supported or resisted a particular Fund policy. Rather than 'going along to get along,' Directors will then have an incentive to register their dissent. Like it or not, consensus and compromise are the enemies of accountability.

The Fund could follow the precedent of the Monetary Policy Committee of the Bank of England, the US Federal Reserve Board's Open Market Committee and the Policy Board of the Bank of Japan, which take formal votes and make public the voting record of each of its members with a short lag. The individual voting records of the members of the Bank of England's Monetary Policy Committee are published after two weeks; those of members of the Federal Reserve Board's Open Market Committee after five to seven weeks; and those of the Bank of Japan's Policy Board after eight weeks. There is no reason why the IMF could not follow suit.

Releasing information about the voting records of the Executive Board, it might be objected, will subject Board members to undue political influence from their national constituencies. One answer is that political influence is inevitable – indeed, it is desirable in the view of those who argue for greater accountability – but it should be exercised by political outsiders as well as by political insiders (following Buiter, 1999). Only if the votes of their representatives are made public can outsiders realistically have a say. The alternative is for members of the Board to be made independent and insulated from undue political influence, as we argue below.

4.3.3 **Publication of minutes**

Accountability would be further enhanced if Directors were required to articulate the rationale for their decisions and if the substance of their statements were made public. At present, the chairman's summary of Board discussions (reproduced in the Fund's Annual Report) provides only a highly compressed and sanitized version of the give-and-take. The Fund should instead report the statements and positions of individual Directors so that their ultimate constituencies – the public of the countries they represent – can better assess whether their interests are being properly represented. It could follow the precedent of the Federal Reserve Board's Open Market Committee, for example, by releasing lightly edited minutes of its deliberations with a lag of five weeks.

While these reforms would be useful, it is important to be realistic about what they can achieve. There is the danger that meaningful discussion and decision-making will shift to the cloakroom and that Directors will appear in the Board only to make uncontroversial statements after disagreements have been hashed out and side deals cut in private.

That said, the precedent of national central banks that take formal votes and release minutes does suggest that such procedures, if implemented in a measured way, can enhance accountability. This suggests following the examples of the Bank of England and the Bank of Japan, which do not attribute particular arguments to particular board members. Instead, they publish minutes presenting key facts and considerations that determined how each board member voted and which, in the case of the Bank of Japan, provide attributed explanations for dissenting votes.

4.3.4 Self-evaluation of programmes

Finally, accountability of staff and management can be enhanced if the Fund regularizes the process of commissioning staff evaluations of each of its programmes and making them publicly available. This is something it already does in controversial, highly visible cases, as with its 'Lessons from the Asian Crisis' paper, which after being discussed by the Board was posted on the internet. In the future, self-evaluations should be obligatory, with the process regularized and publication not at the discretion of the Board, as it is at present.

In this context, there is the question of whether IMF staff charged with undertaking these self-evaluations can reach conclusions that are critical of the institution. Governments can pass laws protecting 'whistle-blowers' from dismissal, but this does not mean that whistle-blowers continue to be promoted up through the ranks.

The implication is that outside evaluations of the Fund's activities are essential, and the practice of commissioning them should be expanded and regularized. At present, the Board commissions *ad hoc* evaluations by independent experts of specific issues like the Highly-Indebted Poor Country initiative, the organization of surveillance, and the Fund's research activities. Regularizing this would mean commissioning annual assessments of each of the Fund's core responsibilities (Article IV surveillance, programmes for crisis countries, etc.) by rotating committees of outside experts, who are granted full access to Fund staff and management and to the institution's internal documentation.

4.3.5 Possible objections

Some will object that releasing information about disagreements in the Board and within the Fund more generally could compound crises. The role of the Fund is to help to restore confidence, and the news that a razor-thin majority of Board members supported a programme, over the objections of a substantial minority, might undermine the catalytic role of IMF intervention. This will create particular anxiety for those wishing to encourage private sector burden sharing – that is, to get private financial institutions to roll over their credit lines to a crisis country and extend new finance. The revelation that respected members of the Board doubted the adequacy of the adjustment measures agreed to by the government and the Fund would hardly encourage private sector forbearance.

Those who warn of these dangers have a point. But no one proposes to televise Executive Board debates and votes. The proposal is rather to release information after a delay of a few weeks or months. By that time, representatives of the country will have had the opportunity to meet the representatives of the major international banks and renegotiate credit lines. Governments will have had time to prepare their case and defend their positions.

It might be objected that accumulating policy credibility is a long, drawn-out process, and that releasing information about disagreements within the Executive Board may damage the credibility of a programme even if release is delayed. The counter-argument is that it is unrealistic to assume that the reservations of Directors and their governments can be kept secret forever.[35] If the news that there are reservations within the Board about the adequacy of an adjustment programme hits the market all at once, it can provoke a violent reaction. If on the other hand, information is allowed to filter out gradually, asset prices and associated quantities can adjust more smoothly. This is the optimal way for information to come to the markets over time, and it is exactly what would be achieved with the proposal of releasing formal votes and increasing transparency.

Another objection is that releasing too much information about internal decision-making can create moral hazard. The argument is that just as national central banks cultivate constructive ambiguity to prevent markets from banking on their actions, there is the danger that a highly transparent IMF will become highly predictable, allowing markets and governments to act in anticipation of its responses, perhaps taking additional risks where they feel that they can count on an IMF bail-out.

This criticism has been levied against the policy of openness of the Monetary Policy Committee of the Bank of England. It is said that the markets focus excessively on the votes and statements of individual members and over-react to changes. This is an argument for retaining at least a degree of opacity in decision-making. It can be met by building in a reasonable delay between the taking of a vote and the release of the results to the public and by not attributing every argument to an individual.

Furthermore, this is not an argument against all additional release of information. Uninformed speculation about future IMF actions can lead to an even worse allocation of resources than informed discussion, assuming that the Fund is properly concerned about the implications of its own actions for moral hazard. Thus, it may be argued that following the Fund's Mexican and Asian rescues, the markets' belief that the IMF would also come to the rescue of Russia may have encouraged the 'moral hazard play', in which hedge funds and international banks poured funds into Russian GKOs. More transparent statements by members of the Executive Board to the effect that further disbursements for Russia would have been forthcoming only following clear evidence of progress towards solving the underlying financial problems might well have attenuated this moral problem instead of aggravating it.

4.4 Independence of the Executive Board

4.4.1 Motivation

Reforms to facilitate information flows and enhance transparency and accountability are motivated by the assumption that the problem of IMF decision-making is that management and staff pursue objectives different from those that would be advanced by a better informed, more powerful Executive Board. They are also motivated by the view that Directors and other government representatives may pursue agendas different from those of their national constituencies.

A different critique is that excessive weight attached to national interests prevents the Fund from carrying out its social mandate. This might seem like a radical view, but it is implicit in many recent critiques of the Fund:

- It is implicit, for example, in accounts suggesting that the US government persuaded the Fund to agree to continued disbursements for Russia in 1997–8 despite evidence that Russian economic and financial reform was running off the tracks. The United States allegedly wanted to prop up what it perceived as a reform-minded government and was concerned that economic failure would bring to power extremists who could not be trusted with the country's nuclear capability. The implication is that IMF policies were used to further US security objectives.

- Several of the Fund's recent programmes, like those for Mexico, have been criticized as mainly serving the interests of creditor countries. The provision of financial assistance, it is said, allowed foreign portfolio investors to be repaid at the expense of the taxpayers of the crisis country. The implication in this case is that IMF policies were used to advance creditor interests.

- Another such complaint is that the conditions the Fund attached to its Asian programmes – requiring the crisis countries to open their domestic financial markets and distribution systems to foreign competition – did more to serve the interests of developed countries seeking market access than those of the crisis countries themselves.

However legitimate it may be for countries to offer support to others for political or security reasons, the IMF is not the proper vehicle for advancing such agendas. Its role is distorted and its effectiveness is damaged when its goals become mixed and unclear.

4.4.2 Alternative approaches

How one responds to this critique depends on how general one sees the problem:

■ If one sees the problem as excessive US influence, then a partial solution is to reconfigure quotas to eliminate the country's veto power. The next review of IMF quotas could be an appropriate occasion to reduce the voting share of the United States in the Executive Board. In addition, it would be desirable to change the threshold for a supermajority. The IMF Articles of Agreement could be amended to lower the threshold for a supermajority from 85% to 80%.

■ If one sees the problem of the Fund's excessive responsiveness to national agendas as more general (as we do), the obvious solution is to strengthen the independence of the Executive Board. If Directors are too inclined to take advice from their governments, then the Articles of Agreement should be amended to discourage them from so doing. The analogy with central bank independence is direct. The Statute of the European System of Central Banks, for example, prohibits members of the Board of the European Central Bank from taking advice from their governments. There is no reason why the IMF's Articles of Agreement could not follow suit.

4.4.3 Making independence effective

Under our proposal, Directors could still be appointed by national governments or groups of governments, much as central bank governors in some countries are appointed by state or regional governments.[36] But they would be prohibited from taking instructions from those governments. This would prevent Executive Board decisions from being influenced excessively by the parochial interests of national governments.

By itself, statutory independence may not be enough. Effective independence may also require:

■ that the Articles of Agreement be amended to specify that Directors will be appointed to multi-year terms of office;

■ that Directors receive adequate compensation (although experience suggests that this should not be a problem);

■ that the Articles of Agreement be amended to include a provision barring Directors from moving laterally into government or finance for a specified period following their term on the Board (although enforcement of such a provision would not be straightforward);

■ and that the Board enjoys budgetary independence. Directors already have the power to vote for an increase in IMF quotas. But quota increases are an awkward device for increasing the Fund's lending power since most of them accrue to the developed countries. In addition, therefore, it may be desirable for the Board to exercise the option of borrowing from the market.

4.5 Accountability of the Executive Board

Independence is acceptable only if members of the Executive Board, while free to chose their strategies and tactics, are accountable to their constituents and therefore answerable for the decisions they take. Two ways of ensuring accountability of the Board are by giving it an explicit mandate, with reference to which it must justify its decisions, and by giving the Interim Committee of national ministers the power to hold members of the Board responsible for their actions.

4.5.1 An explicit mandate

Giving the members of an independent regulatory agency a mandate to pursue specific social and economic goals is a conventional way of holding them accountable. Thus, members of independent regulatory agencies are commonly given a mandate to ensure adequate competition and to maintain a proper balance between the interests of consumers and producers. The members of independent central bank boards are given a mandate to pursue price stability. If they are unable to justify their actions in terms of that mandate, they may be subject to dismissal, which works to hold them accountable.

An analogous mandate – for example, to advance economic and financial stability – would work similarly to hold the members of an independent Executive Board properly accountable for their actions. Members of the Board would have to justify their actions in terms of this mandate, and if they failed to do so they would be subject to dismissal (through mechanisms we describe below). The mandate could be created by amending the Fund's Articles of Agreement to give Directors this responsibility explicitly.

An objection to this approach is that an effective mandate is more difficult to craft for an international financial institution with many instruments and objectives than it is for, say, an electrical power regulator or a central bank. A utility regulator sets the price of electricity, a central bank the interest rate. The IMF, in contrast, has a plethora of objectives and instruments. It is therefore harder to evaluate a claim that a particular policy is consistent with its mandate for pursuing economic and financial stability.

There is something to this claim, but the contrast with independent agencies at the national level should not be overdrawn. Utility regulators, in fact, concern themselves with a host of other policies besides the prices charged to consumers. Consider, for example, the wide-ranging decisions toward the establishment of product standards and marketing alliances taken by the US Federal Communications Commission in the high-tech sphere. And consider the role of the US Federal Reserve System in bank regulation, policy toward highly leveraged financial institutions and the debate over reform of the international financial architecture. The IMF may possess a varied portfolio of policy instruments and objectives, but the narrowness of the policy mandate given to national central banks and regulators should not be exaggerated.

4.5.2 Accountability to the Interim Committee

Some may remain suspicious that statutory independence for the Board would vest too much power in an all-powerful Board of monetary technocrats. As with an independent central bank, the Board must, in the long run, be held accountable for its actions. Who then would hold the Fund's independent Directors accountable?

The obvious answer is the Interim Committee of finance ministers. In the same way that a national parliament or congress holds independent central bank governors accountable, the finance ministers sitting on the Interim Committee, who are the political representatives of the national governments that are the Board's immediate constituency, would carry out this function. We therefore propose that it should be possible to dismiss individual Directors by a supermajority vote of the Interim Committee.[37]

Recent steps to strengthen Interim Committee oversight of the IMF are consistent with this idea. Building on proposals by the French

Government (detailed in the appendix to this chapter), the G-7 summit in Cologne in June 1999 agreed that the Interim Committee should be given permanent standing and renamed the 'International Financial and Monetary Committee'. Deputy-level meetings of the committee would be held twice a year shortly before ministerial meetings. The President of the World Bank would participate in the deliberations of the committee, while the Chairman of the Financial Stability Forum would enjoy observer status. Joint sessions with the World Bank's Development Committee would be held on issues where there is a clear overlap of responsibilities.

These useful reforms, designed to strengthen the Interim Committee, would better position it to hold an independent IMF Executive Board accountable. They would help to give the Interim Committee the legitimacy it needs to carry out this task.

4.6 Reflections on the proposal

Some readers may be sceptical of our proposal for independence for the Executive Board on the grounds that we are arguing by way of analogy with the case for central bank independence, a case on which doubt has been thrown by recent research (see, for example, Posen, 1995). It is important, therefore, to be clear on how our argument differs. Much of the literature on central bank independence focuses on the time-consistency problem and on the credibility of central bankers' commitment to low inflation (see, for example, Cukierman, 1992). This is not our primary concern. Our motivation has more affinity with the older literature on political business cycles (see Nordhaus, 1975), in which it is argued that governments controlling the levers of policy may be inclined to pursue purely self-serving goals.

But there may be a sense in which a more independent Executive Board can be justified on time-consistency grounds. 'Too-big-to-fail' arguments make it difficult for the IMF to stand back and refuse to assist a country that runs into financial difficulties. Knowing that the Fund will ultimately come to the rescue can therefore be a source of moral hazard for national officials and international investors alike. If the Fund were able to commit credibly to assisting a debtor only under truly exceptional circumstances, that moral hazard would be less.

The problem is that such a commitment, however attractive *ex ante*, may not be attractive *ex post*, as we argued in Chapter 3. There is a temptation to bail out just one more country and leave the problem of moral hazard for another day – just as a central bank is tempted to ratify today's inflation and leave the problem of inflationary expectations to another day.

Delegating policy to an independent Executive Board whose members take this moral hazard problem seriously is one way out of this box. It is analogous to the argument for delegating domestic monetary policy to a conservative central banker whose exceptional aversion to inflation offsets the temptation to follow time-inconsistent policies (see Rogoff, 1985).

Finally, it can be asked of our proposal: is it realistic? Amending the Articles of Agreement to create an independent Executive Board would be a radical change in IMF governance. But in an age when respectable economists and politicians argue for abolishing the institution, ours is a relatively modest proposal. For those who recognize that financial markets do not work perfectly – creating the need for an institution to act as a backstop for the markets – but who at the same time worry that the agendas of national governments too often distort IMF decision-making, it is the logical solution. At the very least, it deserves serious consideration.

APPENDIX A catalogue of proposals for IMF reform

This appendix catalogues existing proposals for strengthening IMF decision-making and enhancing the institution's accountability.

The Miyazawa proposal

The Japanese proposal for reforming IMF decision-making, announced by finance minister Miyazawa in March 1999 has two core components (Miyazawa, 1999):

- First, the Fund should regularly invite officials from crisis countries to participate in Executive Board discussions of the design of the rescue programme.
- Second, the Fund should set up programme committees within the Board to discuss prospective programmes before the staff begins negotiations with the aid recipient.

Both proposals are sensible, but by themselves they would not change much. One can imagine that the Executive Board would be more sensitive to disagreements between IMF staff and management on the one hand and the afflicted government on the other if information about such disagreements was not filtered through the staff report, and/or in the presence of the Executive Director for the constituency that includes the crisis country.

It might also be argued that if the government of the crisis country had a seat at the Board table, Directors would have additional information about country-specific circumstances, the agenda-setting power of staff and management would be less. As Stiglitz (1999) emphasizes, more informed voters are more confident voters; and hence, Directors would have more confidence to register dissenting votes.

At present, it is not clear how much additional information Directors would obtain as a result of seating the crisis country at the Board table. But in an independent IMF, as we propose, it may become very important. Currently, the government in question can already make its views known through the representative of its constituency, but in our proposal, Directors would not be allowed to receive instructions from member countries. This is why it would be desirable for a country under review to send representatives to the Board when its programme is being debated.

The effectiveness of regularly constituted programme subcommittees within the Board, which would meet before the staff commences negotiations with the crisis country, is less evident. If this is intended as a response to the complaint that staff and management are able to present the results of those negotiations as a *fait accompli*, it is not clear that constituting a programme committee would make much difference. Deciding the parameters of a programme requires timely information on country conditions, which can be obtained only through a staff mission.

Discussions between staff and a programme committee of Directors prior to a mission would not change this state of affairs, nor would it do much to overcome this information asymmetry. As for decision-making, a programme committee composed of a subset of Board members could not take decisions about the particulars of the programme.

The Sachs proposal

Jeffrey Sachs (1998) has also proposed changes in the functioning of the IMF Executive Board designed to enhance its oversight of the actions of staff and management. The rationale for his proposals is that a better informed Board will be a more effective overseer of the institution. To this end, he advocates:

- opening Board meetings to the interested public;
- providing opportunities for outside parties to submit evidence to the Board;
- and encouraging Executive Board initiatives to solicit professional opinions from beyond the IMF staff.

Opening Board meetings to the public is no more feasible, in our view, than opening up the meetings of the Open Market Committee of the Federal Reserve Board, given the sensitive nature of its decisions and the proprietary and sensitive nature of much of the information discussed. For this reason, we have argued instead for releasing summaries of Board discussions and votes.

Providing opportunities for outside parties to submit evidence to the Board and creating channels for the Board to solicit professional opinions beyond the staff makes more sense. Both are ways of encouraging a Board that is better informed and can exercise more effective oversight of staff and management.

There is an analogy with the Panel of Academic Consultants meetings convened periodically by the Federal Reserve Board to expose monetary policy-makers to the views of independent experts and limit the agenda-setting power of the chairman and the staff. Similarly, there is an analogy with the congressional hearings through which committees of the US House of Representatives and Senate hear the views of independent experts regarding the decisions taken by public agencies, a process which strengthens their hand when they seek to hold the agencies accountable for their actions.

But these analogies also make clear what can realistically be expected of such initiatives. Recall that Congressional hearings on the rescue of Long Term Capital Management, allowing independent experts to give their views on the advisability of the New York Fed's actions, were convened well after the event. Given the financially sensitive nature of the negotiations and the difficulty of identifying at short notice which potential witnesses had a vested interest and which did not, the House Banking Committee did not call for hearings on the subject while the rescue was still underway.

The role for such testimony is thus to provide perspective and inform future decision-making, not to change the way a current crisis is being handled. Hence, meetings of the Federal Reserve Board's Panel of Academic Consultants are generally concerned with discussion of some special topic of general relevance (such as the implications of European monetary union for the international monetary system, or whether the US economy's underlying rate of productivity growth has changed), and the panel is constituted as such. At the end of each meeting, it is traditional, as a courtesy or an afterthought, to ask the assembled experts whether they have any advice for the Board of Governors on current monetary policy. One could imagine that periodic meetings of an IMF Panel of Academic Consultants would be similarly concerned with special topics like those listed above, and that its members would have an opportunity at the end of the meeting to offer their views on the Fund's recent or prospective programmes.

The Edwards proposal

Sebastian Edwards (1998b) would replace the IMF with a trio of specialized agencies:

- A Global Information Agency, which would concentrate on providing timely and uncensored information on the financial condition of countries. The agency would publish public ratings of domestic financial systems and issue red alerts when countries were not providing it with adequate information.
- A Contingent Global Financial Facility, which would provide contingent credit lines for countries following fundamentally sound policies but with temporary liquidity problems that were certified by the Global Information Agency as complying with its standards.
- A Global Restructuring Agency, which would have the power to impose a stay of payments (for a 'cooling-off period') and would provide official financing, subject to conditionality, for countries that were engaged in good faith negotiations with their creditors and making a realistic effort to restructure their economies.

The problem with creating three separate institutions – some of which would have rating responsibilities to the exclusion of lending functions – is that such institutions would be weak. Not having committed funds to them, countries would have less interest in the workings of such institutions. Nor is it clear that Edwards' Contingent Global Financial Facility would in practice predicate its policy on the ratings provided by his Global Information Agency, since the former was not deciding the ratings itself. Strengthening surveillance and crisis management requires strong institutions that combine these functions.

The French proposal for empowering the Interim Committee

The French government has proposed to increase the decision-making power of the Fund's Interim Committee. The Interim Committee, which has met twice a year since its inception in the early 1970s, provides advice to the IMF, although it has no formal decision-making power. It consists of 24 governors (typically finance ministers) representing the same constituencies as the Executive Board.

Under the French proposal, the Interim Committee would meet more regularly and have more say in the day-to-day affairs of the Fund. In the French view, this formidable group of national finance ministers would counter the tendency for influence over decision-making to drift towards the United States and IMF staff and management.

The practicality of this proposal is dubious. It is far from clear that the Interim Committee could lay down more than the most general guidelines for how the IMF should respond, to the extent that every crisis is different in its particulars and different in particular from the crises that preceded it. Nor could it credibly commit to meet with the regularity required to craft a response to unfolding events.

When a crisis hits, the Executive Board meets continuously over a period of days, hearing staff analyses, questioning management's recommendations, and attempting to reach a consensus. Finance ministers, with many competing demands on their time, would not be able to drop their other responsibilities and travel to Washington whenever an outbreak of market turbulence required.

Since ministers would presumably rely on their deputies, it is not clear that vesting more authority in the Interim Committee would in fact create an effective counterweight to IMF staff and management and US influence. It is not clear, in other words, that the resulting process would be fundamentally different from the current arrangement in which ministers rely on members of the Executive Board as their eyes, ears and mouths.

The French government argues that enhancing the powers of the Interim Committee would also enhance the accountability of the Fund. Insofar as it then would be clear that national governments, in the person of their finance ministers, were taking decisions, the latter would be taken to task in the event that those decisions proved misguided. But the *status quo* is one in which Executive Directors report to and take instructions from precisely those same governments.

It might perhaps be argued that the individual national finance ministers on the Interim Committee are ultimately answerable to individual national governments, which makes them more accountable than Executive Directors, who typically answer to constituencies made up of multiple countries. But if this is the argument, then accountability would be achieved at the expense of representativeness and legitimacy since countries whose finance ministers were not included on the Interim Committee would be excluded.

All in all, it is far from clear why what is essentially a cosmetic change in the administrative hierarchy would result in a real improvement in accountability. Our proposal for granting independence to the Executive Board would actually give more power to the Interim Committee. Indeed, the Interim Committee would have the ultimate responsibility of holding the Executive Board accountable.

The UK proposal

The UK proposal, submitted to European Union finance ministers in Dresden in April 1999, would set up an overarching committee to supervise the IMF's Interim Committee, the World Bank's Development Committee and the newly established Financial Stability Forum, housed at the BIS. This committee would operate at the level of finance ministers and would include the G-7 countries as well as an undetermined number of emerging market countries.

The appeal of this proposal is that financial problems are increasingly interlinked in a world of globalized markets: there is less intellectual justification than there once might have been for separate committees concerned with financial and development problems. In addition, the Fund's growing concern with bank regulation, reform of financial arrangements generally, and other structural matters creates an obvious rationale for closer coordination with the World Bank (which has traditionally been responsible for advising on structural reform) and the BIS (which provides the umbrella for the Basle Committee on Banking Supervision and the newly established Financial Stability Forum). This committee can be seen as an international economic security council.

The intent is clearly to strengthen coordination between the major international financial institutions as well as to enhance political control. An additional objective is to give some additional weight to the emerging countries, which have become the major beneficiaries of IMF packages. All these are worthy aims but it seems that such a council will not have the time to exercise effective control over the Fund. By creating a higher-level forum, it will deprive the Interim Committee of some of its authority without establishing a clear relationship with the Fund's Board.

A variant has been put forward by Italy as a compromise between the rival French and UK plans. This 'double-hat' proposal would transform the Interim Committee, adding to its IMF responsibility that of being the overarching body supervising the World Bank and the Financial Stability Forum as well as the regulatory agencies that set international standards.

Whether such reform is worthwhile would hinge on whether a single committee with three subcommittees would really be a fundamental improvement on the present structure of entirely separate committees. If this reorganization led to significantly closer coordination, it would be a good thing. But the qualifier 'significantly' is key.

Nevertheless, the UK proposal does have a key point: reorganizing the Interim Committee to clarify its mandate and enhance its legitimacy is essential if it is to be effective in holding an independent Executive Board accountable.

The Italian proposal

Italian finance minister Ciampi, in his capacity as President of the Interim Committee, has suggested setting up preparatory meetings at the level of Alternates. The intent is to duplicate the procedure that already exists for G-7 and European Union meetings of finance ministers. Lower-level meetings of this type are known to result in more open discussions, and even to more productive negotiations, than meetings at the level of finance ministers. Their conclusions often form the basis of agreements.

This proposal would enhance the ability of the Interim Committee to exercise control over the Fund. It would complement our own suggestion to empower both the Board and the Interim Committee.

The proposal for regional funds

A final set of proposals recommends the creation of regional monetary funds as centres of economic analysis, finance and conditionality competing with the IMF. The idea of an Asia Fund was first advanced by the Japanese government soon after the outbreak of the Asian crisis and the idea has been reiterated subsequently by various academics and officials (see Ito, Ogawa and Sasaki, 1999).

In the same way that market competition disciplines producers, competition in the market for ideas, finance and conditionality would have a disciplining influence on the IMF. Historically, there have been few other sources of influential economic analysis to compete with the IMF's own internal analysis. In the absence of clear alternatives, the Fund's diagnosis of how governments should regulate their international accounts and manage crises has carried the day.

This point should not be exaggerated: the Fund has prominent academic critics, who are not exactly reluctant to express their differences with the IMF line; and other international institutions, like the World Bank and the United Nations Development Programme, have been known to go public about their differences with the Fund – as in the case of World Bank criticism of the use of high interest rates to stabilize depreciating currencies. But the critics do not typically have the ability to link their recommendations to financial assistance in a crisis. It is the Fund that spearheads financial rescues, so it is the Fund's advice that ultimately carries the day.

Thus, one of the arguments for regional monetary funds is that they can provide both a financial and intellectual counterweight. If countries in crisis could appeal to both the IMF and their regional monetary fund for advice and assistance (and that assistance was, therefore, conditioned on different policy actions by the government in question), there would then be a genuine competition between ideas. This is presumably one of the considerations the Japanese government had in mind when it tabled its proposal for an Asian fund.

In a competitive economy, the firm with the best ideas produces the best product, makes the most profits and ends up dominating its market segment. But it is not clear that this analogy carries over to the market for policy advice and international financial assistance. Proponents of the idea of competing monetary funds would perhaps argue that regional funds that offer inferior policy advice will not find their recommendations followed and their financial assistance solicited. As a consequence, their influence and market share will be eroded. For example, if it had a poorer understanding of the roots of the Asian crisis and what measures should be taken to address it than experts employed by an Asia Fund based in, say Tokyo, then the IMF would lose business to its regional competitor.

In practice, it is questionable whether international financial institutions behave like profit-maximizing firms. It does not follow that an institution that offers inferior advice ends up not being repaid and is forced to file for bankruptcy. The IMF is paid before other creditors because of its signalling function. (Historically, it is almost always paid back promptly.) It is not likely that a regional fund that lent to governments at unrealistically low interest rates would be driven out of business, since it could always have its coffers replenished by the high-income countries that were its principal shareholders.

This points to the obvious danger that political considerations will weigh at least as heavily in the lending decisions of any new regional funds as they do in those of the IMF. The availability and terms of financial assistance extended by regional funds may be even more heavily driven by non-economic considerations (such as maintenance of the political *status quo*) to the extent that governments are especially worried about political turmoil in their own back yards.

This is one rationale for the IMF's initial opposition to the idea of an Asia fund: that Asian governments, which could appeal to Tokyo for financial assistance, would be able to obtain it without the same pressure to adjust, undercutting IMF conditionality. Indeed, regional funds would be even more prone to political capture than global institutions.

Thus, whether the proliferation of regional monetary funds enhanced the efficiency of the market for policy advice would ultimately depend on whether the lending decisions of those funds were driven by economic analysis or politics. This is an argument for structuring operations of any new regional funds so as to insulate them from political pressures. Like the members of the Board of the European Central Bank, their board members could be appointed to long terms in office and, in principle, be prohibited from taking advice from their national governments. Of course, the enforceability of such arrangements is questionable. And this degree of autonomy for the directors of international financial institutions would be a step backwards in terms of accountability. This is not a dilemma that is easily finessed.

There may be other good arguments for regional monetary funds. But it is not clear that they would really create a more competitive market for ideas. A better solution would be to enhance the efficiency of the IMF by strengthening its transparency, independence and accountability.

Discussions and Roundtables

Discussion of Chapters 1 and 2

How has the IMF Managed the 'New' Crises?

Jon Cunliffe
HM Treasury, London
Jon Cunliffe was not convinced that all the financial crises since Mexico have really been so new. The Asian crises had their origins in a combination of huge capital inflows, over-investment and banking sector problems. The Brazilian crisis, on the other hand, was more old-fashioned with fiscal imbalances as the main driving force. And even if the crises occurred in the context of a world of liberalized capital markets, issues like proper legislation and supervision loomed large.

Cunliffe thought that the Report was too Fund-centred and that it overlooked the role of other international surveillance and regulatory institutions. At the domestic level, the rule of law, codes of conduct, and government action provide the public good of financial stability. How can this public good be provided at the international level without an international government? Few would propose a supranational institution to regulate financial markets, so the development of standards and codes of conduct is absolutely crucial. But effective international surveillance and supervision are very difficult to implement. The fundamental problem is to create the right incentives.

Therefore, the central questions are: What is the best way to increase coordination among national and international supervisory authorities and the international financial institutions? What is the role of the IMF? Should we give it more leverage? How can we get the IMF operational at the early stage of an emerging

105

crisis? The establishment of the new Contingent Credit Line (CCL) is the most important achievement in the last few years. The increase in transparency is equally important. The IMF has a central role in surveillance but how will it deliver this surveillance? And when the Fund detects a problem, should it be made public, and if so, when?

With respect to crisis resolution, Cunliffe observed that the Report barely mentioned the function of lender of last resort. Giving the IMF such a function would be extremely difficult. What can be done in the absence of an international lender of last resort? Cunliffe advocated the involvement of the private sector, both to prevent moral hazard and because of the size of the resources required. But important questions remain: Does the IMF need other tools to involve the private sector? And how can the IMF and the international community credibly pre-commit themselves to the use of certain tools?

Flemming Larsen
International Monetary Fund

Flemming Larsen thought that the Report generalizes too much and that one should look at each crisis separately. In Thailand, for example, the IMF privately issued warnings early on, noting both overheating and large and unsustainable balance of payments deficits. Similarly, the IMF warned Indonesia and Malaysia of important vulnerabilities early on. The Russian crisis may not have been inevitable, but capital flight and overvaluation had become of growing concern. The Brazilian crisis was no surprise – and it was quite traditional: large fiscal imbalances, overvaluation and political uncertainty. The Korean crisis is the one where the IMF probably has the most to learn. Here as well there had been vulnerabilities such as over investment, financial fragilities and a highly leveraged corporate sector, yet the IMF clearly did not foresee this crisis.

What are the most important lessons for the IMF?

- First, Larsen argued, the Fund has not been sufficiently concerned with the potentially destabilizing effect of capital flows, especially short-term flows.
- Second, the IMF has not focused enough on the supply side of capital flows. It must improve its knowledge of financial markets in mature economies and of the interaction of capital

flows with business cycles. It is now clear that the emerging markets would not have faced large net inflows in the 1990s in the absence of protracted recessions in Europe and Japan in the early part of the 1990s. It is equally apparent that the United States has benefited from the reallocation of these funds over the last couple of years. The role of push factors is a crucial element in the understanding of these crises.

- Third, the IMF has not paid enough attention to the asymmetry of capital account liberalization in emerging markets. Often, the crisis countries have encouraged capital inflows from foreign investors but discouraged residents to invest abroad. The IMF should encourage national authorities to reform their national banking and financial sector in order to allocate domestic savings efficiently instead of relying on foreign savings. In this regard, strengthening prudential regulation is crucial.

Eventually, the IMF can, and should, do a better job at surveillance. It has been too slow to address structural problems that affect the ability of a country to adjust. Larsen would have liked the Report to be clearer about the extent of IMF involvement in structural reforms. In his opinion, the Fund should, for example, look at balance sheets of the corporate sector. With respect to the more traditional macroeconomic part of surveillance, he was not so sure that the IMF's model is really wrong. As he saw it, fiscal tightening in the Asian countries was not designed to alleviate the current account deficit but to finance the rescue of the banking system. And these countries were in any case very reluctant to loosen fiscal policy. As for monetary policy, Larsen was convinced that higher interest rates are inevitable when a country suffers from a run on its currency.

Is the IMF responsible for the crises? Larsen observed that Malaysia did not follow the Fund's advice and nevertheless went into crisis, and now seems to be recovering more slowly than, for example, Thailand and Korea. Did the IMF lend too much? He did not think so since lower levels of assistance would probably have worsened the crises and exacerbated contagion. Compared with the growth of world GDP and capital flows over the last decades, the Fund's lending capacity has in fact declined.

General Discussion

Hans-Jörg Rudloff agreed with Jon Cunliffe that the recent crises are neither new nor particularly 'high-tech'. They are what they always have been, and should have been forecast. It is essentially a story of hot money. Capital flows are like a bicycle fitted with a jet engine: it takes off fabulously but inevitably ends up crashing. This raises the question of whether the IMF should promote capital account liberalization. What must be enhanced is prudential regulation. Free capital flows without adequate prudential regulation must result in financial crises. In this context, Rudloff was worried by his perception of a general weakening of governance and contractual relations in international finance. Another problem with the IMF is that it is too heavily influenced by the US Treasury.

Andrew Crockett came back to Larsen's argument that fiscal tightening in the Asian countries was not used to alleviate the current account but to recapitalize banks. He wanted to hear the IMF comment on the use of current fiscal revenues to finance already incurred losses.

Giovanni Colombo asked what was the Report's rationale for relating IMF voting shares to trade since this seems to contradict the authors' emphasis on the capital account rather than the current account. He was also unsure about the authors' opinion as to whether the relationship between crises and fundamentals still exists.

Guillermo Perry disagreed with the Report's assessment of early warning systems. As long as they perform better than just flipping a coin – which they typically do – they can be extremely useful in indicating possible future crises. He thought that the establishment of the CCL was a positive achievement. He also emphasized the importance of different initial conditions when the Fund intervenes in a country suffering from a crisis.

Alexander Swoboda said that he had always been profoundly puzzled by the objective of early warning indicator systems. If they really worked, crises would be prevented and it would be impossible to find any statistically significant relationship between the crises and their indicators.

Claudio Segré argued that the debate suffers from confusion between causes and symptoms. Fundamentals are the important factor and they must be examined and, if necessary, corrected instead of blaming capital flows resulting from flawed economic policies.

Giorgio Gomel thought that the Report does not distinguish clearly between the rule-making and rule enforcement functions in the international area. The former should be left to specialized technical and self-regulatory bodies (such as the Basle Committee and IOSCO) while the latter should belong to the IMF as a part of its surveillance function. Given its universal membership, the IMF has the political legitimacy to push forward the setting of new international rules, standards and codes of conduct. In this connection, the Italian 'double hat' proposal for strengthening the Interim Committee's process of decision-making has clear advantages. According to this proposal, under 'one hat', the Interim Committee would manage purely IMF business prepared by the staff and the Executive Board; while under the 'second hat', it would discuss and make recommendations on issues of wider concern to the world financial system with a broader range of participants.

Richard Portes argued that the CCL suffers from an incentive problem: how can a country be withdrawn from the list? He also commented on the early warning literature. This is an old story that started in the early 1970s. Even though we now have more and better data and unimaginably higher computing power, we have not been able to overcome the fundamental trade-off between Type I and Type II errors. With respect to the Russian and Brazilian crises, he asked: did we not all know that both rescue packages would fail? Why then did the Fund put such an amount of money into both operations? Finally, he expressed doubts about the credibility of an international regulator. At the national level, we have institutions that deal with corporate failures and effective enforcement mechanisms: how could the IMF be credible as an international regulator where all of this is absent?

Takatoshi Ito responded to the question of whether it was bad fundamentals that caused the crises or something else. It is very difficult to explain the huge devaluations and capital outflows in the recent crises just on the basis of mere fundamentals and policy mismanagement. Fundamentals and policy failures were not that bad. For example, when Mexico floated the peso, it lost value at an enormous speed. When the IMF came in, the peso had already lost 50% of its value. Correcting the fundamentals could not stop the outflows. This was equally true in Thailand and Indonesia. Thailand first devalued by 15%, then it went down by a further 50% after the Fund had come in. Indonesia did not use up its reserves when it floated the rupiah, the fundamentals were relatively strong, and reforms were under way. Nevertheless, Indonesia experienced the worst devaluation, losing more than 80% of the rupiah's value. Capital flows simply turned crazy. Fundamentals played a role, but new aspects are clearly more important.

José De Gregorio enumerated the list of new potential 'vulnerabilities': the maturity structure of liabilities, the currency mismatch of assets and liabilities, the health of the banking sector and corporate governance. He emphasized the importance of developing international standards and charging the right institutions with their implementation.

Flemming Larsen returned to some of the issues raised by other participants. He first observed confusion about what the political masters want the IMF to do. He fully agreed that it is undesirable that the Fund bails out the private sector, but it may be difficult to avoid this problem completely given the overriding systemic concern about limiting contagion. Second, answering Andrew Crockett, he admitted that the rescue of Asian banks could have been financed by borrowing rather than by current revenues, so that tightening fiscal policy was probably a mistake. But it is doubtful whether these countries could have avoided recession given their problems of over investment, bad loans, etc. In any case, the easing of fiscal policy very early after the initial programmes had been designed meant that fiscal policies had been strongly expansionary in 1998.

While, in Larsen's view, early warning systems are unlikely to predict accurately the timing of a crisis, they are useful for identifying vulnerabilities. In Russia, for example, the risk premia in financial markets were clearly indicating a problem. Brazil was a similar story. More or less all vulnerability indicators had been flashing well in advance, and yet Brazil refused to devalue because it feared that its successful price stabilization programme would be undermined. The shareholders of the IMF accepted this argument and provided the money.

Regarding involvement of the private sector, Larsen observed that private money is still being withdrawn from crisis countries. Finally, he admitted that the criteria required for the CCL might be so restrictive that only countries that do not need them will qualify. This led him to wonder whether any country will apply, or whether, as suggested by the Financial Times, 'it is not a club any of those invited would wish to join'.

Discussion of Chapters 3 and 4

Proposal for Reforming the IMF

Benoît Coeuré
Ministry of Economics and Finance, France
Benoît Coeuré began by noting that a central issue was how to organize the flow of information between IMF staff, the Executive Board, the Interim Committee and the public at large. In this respect, the publication of minutes brings up the conflict inherent in the IMF's two roles as private counsellor and as provider of economic information.

Regarding the Report's proposed independence of the Executive Board, he felt that the opposite case could be made: the Fund needs more, not less, political guidance. It is true that shareholders pursue national agendas but in reality, hidden agendas are the essence of politics. The question, therefore, is whether the problems they create are of first or second order of magnitude. The case has yet to be made. Furthermore, the Executive Directors already form a fairly independent and coherent body, making any strengthening of their independence unnecessary.

Some countries that disagree with the Fund's agenda would consider it compatible with their national agenda if only it dealt with negative externalities. But the scope for reform is fairly limited here. Analogous to a central bank, Board members already have collective thinking, and there may be a need for more national views.

In discussing the mandate of the Fund, and taking account of the political dimensions, three approaches are conceivable:

■ The macroeconomic approach: limit the Fund's mandate to macroeconomic policies (as in Feldstein, 1998). This is an illusory ambition since macroeconomic policies and structural imbalances are intertwined.

- The internal approach: considering the issue of time-consistency, define a clear mandate for the IMF. Comparisons with central banks may be misleading as they never deal with structural aspects while the IMF covers a wider range of issues. But the attributions of the Interim Committee in relation to those of the Executive Board are difficult to set up.

- The external approach: increase political guidance in order to anticipate the structural consequences. The role of the Interim Committee should be reinforced to allow for further political guidance.

Yung Chul Park
Korea University and Korea Exchange Bank

The authors' proposals were not forward looking enough for Yung Chul Park. In the future, the IMF will primarily deal with emerging market and developing economies. It has the structure of a credit union, taking deposits from and making loans to members, but the lenders and the depositors are different in the case of the IMF. To redress this imbalance, developing countries should be asked to contribute more resources and to have a larger voice in the IMF so that they be properly represented. For the IMF to be able to enforce its decisions, the issue of representation definitely has to be tackled first. In the same vein, international standards enforced by the IMF must recognize that standards set for the developed countries do not necessarily fit the needs of developing countries.

Park also took issue with the Report's criticism of regional funds. To start with, crises are mostly regional. In addition, lenders and creditors are also often from the same region. Both the setting of standards and the handling of crises are likely to be dealt with more efficiently at the regional than at the international level. That a regional arrangement could be a complement to the IMF should not simply be dismissecd. For example, regional funds could start as subsidiaries of the IMF.

As a result of liberalization of the capital account and the related increase in capital flows, many emerging market economies find it necessary to hold a larger amount of foreign exchange reserves than before, even though they are on a floating exchange rate system. For example, Korean authorities are targeting a level of reserves equivalent to 20% of GDP. Holding such a large amount of reserves is costly and obviously represents a misallocation of resources.

Regional monetary arrangements could pool together the reserves of their member countries to create regional contingency credit facilities. These facilities would allow the member countries to hold, on average, a smaller amount of reserves than otherwise and develop common defences against future financial crises within the region.

In many emerging market economies, the flexible exchange rate system is not working as well as expected. This is because policy authorities are extremely reluctant to allow large fluctuations in the nominal exchange rate, that is, a high degree of volatility of the real exchange rate in the short run. For this reason, monetary policy is often geared to stabilize the nominal exchange rate. To gain monetary autonomy, therefore, these countries will be forced to control short-term capital movements.

Finally, Park reminded the audience that at the IMF annual meetings in Hong Kong in the autumn of 1997, most discussions among private investors and the Korean authorities centred around the existence of an implicit government guarantee for private debts. The IMF did not seem to be aware of that, and discovered the problem in the midst of the crisis a few weeks later. This is an illustration of the need for the Fund to provide more analysis and information on international financial markets and institutions, including structural changes as well as current trends, to emerging market economy policy-makers.

General Discussion
Jean-Pierre Landau emphasized the need for an international institution that is able to provide large amounts of liquidity at very short notice. Such an institution would be instrumental in coping with the negative consequences of contagion. The immediate effect of contagion – and the source of ensuing damages – is a sudden shortage of liquidity. In the case of emerging market economies, the liquidity effects of contagion are particularly severe. The major reason is a substantial asymmetry of size between investors and borrowers. What is a modest portfolio reallocation for creditors may represent a massive drain of liquidity that debtor countries' official reserves cannot cushion. Without the provision of emergency external liquidity, developing countries are forced to accumulate reserves by running substantial current account surpluses with inevitable deflationary pressures.

What could the IMF do about this problem? Landau offered three recommendations to speed up the liquidity provision process. First, the provision of liquidity should be subject to a transparent *ex ante* conditionality. Second, there should be a very swift procedure for front-loaded disbursements. Third, more resources should be pooled, for example, via an increase in quotas.

Concerning governance, Landau found the authors' case for an independent IMF rather unconvincing and that it certainly called for further clarifications. The IMF, he argued, is definitely not a central bank. By its very nature, the Fund is political. Furthermore, the Board is already highly flexible and the Fund's policy is generally very responsive to the Board's opinions. Finally, the Board offers the ability to create a political consensus, an essential element that independence would probably threaten. If a reform in governance is needed, Landau concluded, a good idea would be to reconsider the poor design of Article IV.

Nicolas Krul observed that all participants in the discussion systematically presuppose that the IMF will remain the key institution in the international financial system. He viewed this as a severe constraint on imaginative thinking.

Flemming Larsen expressed full agreement with Yung Chul Park's view that the Fund needed a much deeper understanding of the way financial markets really work. Monitoring is not enough. It should be posssible to anticipate better the problems to which financial markets might react. This calls for continuing consultations on structural problems even though these issues often have very serious political implications.

In that respect, Larsen said, the OECD experience may provide a useful benchmark. It was within the OECD forum that the developed countries started to realize that structural issues were central to their current economic problems. This created an impetus for gradual structural reform based on peer pressure and policy cooperation. Emerging market economies need a similar model, possibly at the regional level. The Fund's current consultation model is insufficient to provide the right amount of incentives and cooperation on structural measures. The adoption of standards in many structural policy areas should help to address this problem but it is important to involve the emerging market countries fully in the design of standards. Larsen concluded by sharing the general concern about the risk of deflation in economies struck by crises.

José De Gregorio agreed with Jean-Pierre Landau: the Fund is a political institution. But even though the mandate is clearly defined, the Fund should be able to operate free from direct political interference, the condition being that accountability is properly organized.

Klaus Regling expressed doubts about the feasibility of independence for the simple reason that the money comes from the rich countries. As the main shareholders of the Fund, they are the key decision-makers. It is doubtful that these countries will agree to abandon any direct control on the Fund's actions. Regling also warned against the idea of having the Fund assume an explicit function as lender of last resort. He recalled the intrinsic unsustainability of any commitment to bail out countries. Such a commitment generates more moral hazard that sooner or later materializes into more bail-out operations. He concluded that there was no other way out except to involve the private sector in one way or another in the general concern for financial stability.

Pablo Guidotti commented on the idea of the Fund's independence. He recalled two key elements. First, the Fund is intimately linked to policy-makers – this is precisely where it derives its power from. Second, institutional independence can only be granted on the presumption that dependence on national policy-makers generates distortions in the decision process. He wondered what precisely are the distortions in the present case. Is there any clearly identified bias in the national agendas? Should independence lead to more or less lending? Given the lack of clarity in the nature of the distortions, it is not certain that independence would deliver a more efficient system. Finally, if independence is supposed to solve some time-inconsistency problem, it must not be forgotten that it generally tends to displace the problem rather than solve it.

Takatoshi Ito advocated the 'depoliticization' of the Fund and gave some examples of distortions. Generally speaking, the interference of national agendas in the Fund's actions implies that the latter tend to reflect the interests of the lenders while an institution like the IMF should primarily act in the interests of the borrowers. National agendas should be dealt with through bilateral help. Why do some countries benefit from large IMF rescue packages with loose conditionality while others are either denied a large package or given one with stringent conditionality? Another example of inefficiencies linked to politicization is the CCL: which country will really benefit from it?

Charles Wyplosz put forward three points in favour of the independence proposal:

- First, it is true that independence requires a clearly defined mandate. The present mandate of the Fund is certainly too broad and seriously needs to be refocused.
- Second, the argument that 'the Fund is a political institution anyway' is pointless. Everyone agrees that central banks are also deeply political, but nobody says that granting them independence is the wrong thing to do. Once the mandate is transparent and accountability is ensured, there is no doubt that independence is good.
- Third, recent years provide clear evidence that the Fund's mistakes have the same origin: political interference. The decision to help Russia just before the rouble's collapse in 1998 is, in Wyplosz's view, a dramatically illustrative example.

Klaus Regling briefly came back on the function of lender of last resort and emphasized the fact that rescue operations needed to be unpredictable if one wanted to avoid time-inconsistency problems. He then turned again to the independence proposal. Given that an international institution like the IMF is designed to defend the public good, he wondered how this could be dealt with without involving politics. The IMF is there to respond to political needs. He concluded by warning that the failures evoked by Charles Wyplosz should not mask the fact that, overall, the present system works.

Flemming Larsen insisted on the importance of formal analysis serving as a basis for efficient decisions. He mentioned the merits of the internal review process through which every IMF paper containing policy recommendations is reviewed at various levels. Such a system makes the management aware of disagreement among staff members and contributes to better decisions.

Jean-Pierre Roth recalled that the IMF is using public money. As a result, it needs political control. Moreover, any rescue operation, be it at the national or international level, is essentially a political choice. He agreed that political interference might be a source of inefficiency. But granting independence is going too far given that there exist other mechanisms to limit interference (for example, transparency in the decision-making process).

Barry Eichengreen concluded from the discussion that the Fund would certainly remain at the centre of financial affairs in the foreseeable future. One of its major goals should be to create another way to deal with large-scale crises originating in the capital account. Another crucial issue would be to deal with the moral hazard problem associated with any perceived or effective role of the Fund as lender of last resort. Finally, he was not warm to the idea that the Fund should provide specific information on the way capital markets perceive the situation of a given country. It is much better, he claimed, if the country itself talks to the markets in a clear and direct way.

Yung Chul Park drew two important lessons regarding the feasibility of desirable reforms. Structural conditions, such as minimum standards for corporate governance or accounting, are extremely hard to design and it is not clear that the IMF is well-equipped to face those challenges. As far as independence is concerned, feasibility is also problematic given the dramatic loss of power it would imply for today's decision-makers, the United States and the European Union.

First Panel Discussion

Who Should Pay for the Crises?

Andrew Crockett
Bank for International Settlements

Andrew Crockett emphasized the fact that the international financial system needs not only rules but also guidelines for when contracts cannot be enforced. In periods of crisis, clear bankruptcy rules are required. Internal debates also draw the attention towards bankruptcy laws.

The IMF's role is to minimize the international costs of financial crises. The mechanism by which a country was asked to adjust in order for the IMF to provide funding worked well during the 1950s and 1960s. But nowadays, there is a third actor in the crisis picture: international financial institutions and governments are now joined by private lenders. Equity holders already contribute significantly to the adjustment while bondholders have yet to be brought in. The international community smooths crises, but the existing arrangements are rather unsatisfactory. Cross-border transactions are too numerous and there is a lack of political will to broaden the basis for crisis resolution.

It is, therefore, high time to raise the issue of private sector involvement. How should the private sector contribute? And more importantly, how should it be bailed in? A new design should be agreed after discussion with the private sector. Crockett suggested that the terms on which private actors are bailed in needs to be established *ex ante*. This requires that loan contracts explicitly incorporate adequate clauses and that legal procedures be arranged.

Philipp Hildebrand
Moore Capital Strategy Group

Philipp Hildebrand asserted that the *status quo* is neither satisfactory nor efficient – and is certainly not market-friendly. During the recent crises in Asia and Russia, private investors suffered huge losses (up to US $350 billion). In the case of Russia, the market clearly made a bet – the so-called 'moral hazard play'. For the moment, global solutions favour bondholders against equity investors, which creates a bias towards debt and against foreign direct investment and equity. This *status quo* contributes to the boom–bust cycles in developing countries.

Hildebrand underlined the need for a precautionary system in which the private sector would share the burden. But reforms do not come for free. What could be these costs and who will have to bear them? Developing countries might have to be prepared to accept lower growth while the G-7, the IMF and particularly the United States, should recognize that their influence will decline if crises become less frequent and more benign. This should be recognized and accepted *ex ante*. For example, the 1996 proposal by the G-10 or the 1997 proposal by the G-22 to increase transparency, curtail short-term lending and establish steering committees of creditors, could be reconsidered. Should these proposals be implemented, funding costs might rise marginally but this should be set against the likely reduction of crisis costs. A crucial question is whether capital markets have now sufficiently stabilized to face the costs of implementing such measures at this juncture.

In this connection, Hildenbrand stressed three observations:

- Markets are adaptable. Much as they adjusted to huge boom–bust cycles, they can deal with the more precautionary system that these proposals envision.
- There is much resistance, including in financial markets, to the introduction of bond clauses. Yet if the G-7 takes the lead, the overall reaction of markets will be limited.
- Now is a window of opportunity and this window is unlikely to last for long. The financial system is getting back on its feet and huge capital flows will have already resumed, especially towards developing countries. Once this happens, support for reform will quickly dwindle.

Richard Portes
Centre for Economic Policy Research and London Business School

Richard Portes started by noting that banks rarely lose money in crises and that capital markets have very short memory. Who has paid for the crises over the previous decades? In the 1920s and 1930s, it was bondholders who incurred losses. In the 1970s and 1980s, banks did not lose money (on average). Mexico suffered terms-of-trade losses, and the population was affected. In Asia, losses were related to bank loans, terms-of-trade losses, equity and real estate and unemployment. In Russia, there were big losers but also huge gainers among banks.

The discrepancy between who *actually* pays the costs of crises and those who *should* pay them is vast: the burden should be shared between creditors and debtors. While the IMF's role is to provide liquidity assistance, creditors and debtors need to be provided with fair burden-sharing arrangements. In particular, careful lessons should be drawn from the recent bail-outs financed with public money: there is no good reason why ordinary taxpayers should pay these costs of financial intermediation.

When a crisis erupts, the IMF must step in and pull the plug. But without bailout arrangements, it is nearly impossible to do so. Debt contracts ought to recognize the risk of failure and adequate clauses must be introduced in bond markets. Why is this not happening? The private sector fights, and will continue to fight, against bail-ins. They argue that the costs are too high and will want the volume disbursed to be lower. There has been no substantial change in official reports from 1996 to 1999, nor is there a need for change. It is pointless to await private creditor proposals.

Guillermo Perry
World Bank

Guillermo Perry focused first on the effects of financial crises on the poor. The poor are less adaptable due to a lack of human capital, physical or financial assets. They cannot smooth consumption and therefore suffer disproportionately. As political instability rises, the number of school drop-outs increases and the efficiency of the social safety net declines. The poor are the silent voice in the current debate. To counter this huge market failure, the IMF and the World Bank will have to act counter-cyclically, much more than they have done in the past.

Gradually involving the private sector in preventing and solving crises would help reduce liquidity risks. But dealing efficiently with crises requires both an *ex ante* and an *ex post* strategy:

Ex ante, we need the CCL or some form of precautionary buffer, private support and official guarantees, debt insurance and call options. While it is unrealistic to expect that official guarantees will always come in a counter-cyclical manner, some kind of institutionalization is needed. This may include burden-sharing measures, such as bankruptcy provisions and bond covenants. While this is now well understood and usually accepted, nothing will happen until the OECD countries pave the way.

Ex-post measures for bailing in and burden sharing must include roll-overs and debt restructuring. Roll-overs need to be concerted, which requires new mechanisms to declare and organize stand-stills. As for debt restructuring, the recent experiences in Ukraine and Pakistan have shown, once again, how messy they can be in the absence of adequate clauses. Currently, Ecuador faces huge risks with respect to both domestic deposits and its external debt, with the possibility of contagion unless a solution is quickly found.

General Discussion

Hans-Jörg Rudloff observed that the private sector consists of many elements, there is no such thing as the 'private sector'. He disagreed with bailing in proposals because they do not really ease restructuring. Instead, there should be more public discussion about losses, closer surveillance and compliance. The private sector should find its preferred solution.

Further exchanges stressed the lack of conclusiveness of current debates. In particular, little has been said of the implications of possible reforms of bond contracts on IMF policies. This leaves a huge amount of uncertainty regarding the behaviour of officials in the event of a new crisis.

Second Panel Discussion

Does the IMF need Reform?

Pablo Guidotti
Ministry of Economics, Argentina

Pablo Guidotti initially observed that at least on the basis of Argentina's experience, globalization and the opening of capital accounts have been beneficial for the emerging market countries. There have been costs in terms of increased volatility but the balance is unambiguously positive.

Regarding the role of the IMF, whose role during good times is mainly policy advice and policy design, he thought that it had been successful in the area of fiscal policy, but less so in monetary and exchange rate policy. This partly reflects the fact that it is easier to achieve consensus on fiscal issues. The Fund has now entered new areas, mainly banking and structural policies. Banking supervision is not an area where the Fund is likely to develop a comparative advantage, so it might not be a good idea to encourage an extension of its mandate. As for structural policies, clearly the IMF has not yet developed its doctrine, but is learning as it goes.

During bad times, the main role of the IMF is to provide liquidity to avoid crashes. In this task, it is hampered by the large number of currencies and by the role of financial markets as a continuous source of shocks. The best approach is to improve *ex ante* surveillance, mainly by avoiding too short a maturity of foreign debt and too rigid exchange rate regimes.

There is no doubt that the Fund will remain at the centre of the international financial system, but in order to improve its performance, it has to reform its internal organization. It should not be the only forum where issues regarding the world monetary system are tackled. Over the years, we will need to establish other fora for discussions between the rich and poor countries. The Financial Stability Forum is a step in the right direction. In addition, the IMF's current constituency system no longer represents the evolution of the international financial system. This weakens the Executive Board in particular, and more generally the Fund's authority.

Klaus Regling
Moore Capital Strategy Group

The main role of the Fund is to decrease the frequency and depth of crises. What are the reforms needed to reach this target? First, Klaus Regling stated, independence of the Fund is the wrong issue. Independence makes sense for central banks at the national level but not at the international level because the IMF has a much wider mandate than a central bank, including fiscal and structural issues. Also, the function of lender of last resort should not be moved from the national to the international level. It is entirely appropriate that Board members represent the point of view of their governments. But that does not mean that the Fund has to be weak.

Moreover, there exists a special role for the G-7 (G-8) in this context. This was clear in the Korean, Brazilian and Russian crises. Regling admitted the existence of a trade-off between transparency and efficiency, but he observed that in a crisis, the IMF must act rapidly, which inevitably reduces transparency. The solution, he suggested, is for the Fund to explain clearly the reasons for its actions.

Over the years, the IMF has developed a wide variety of facilities. This is unhelpful and a source of unnecessary complexity. The truth is that most finance ministers do not understand, nor do they care for, the nuances between the facilities. Some streamlining is clearly required.

On the issue of conditionality, Regling said that the Fund's performance is by and large satisfactory. The only serious criticism is that some conditions are occasionally too ambitious. As they are not met, there is a loss of effectiveness and credibility.

For the immediate future, Regling thought that the Fund's main challenge is to find ways to deal with excessive short-term capital flows. These flows played a crucial role in recent crises. He offered a few guiding principles:

- There should be no more bail-outs. The IMF could develop its recently adopted practice of lending into arrears. It should have the right to impose standstills.
- Countries should be encouraged to adopt more flexible exchange rate regimes.
- The emphasis should be on market-based approaches in many

domains: discouraging short-term capital flows and decreasing their volatility – possibly through Chilean-type restrictions on inflows, better debt management, bailing in the private sector and encouraging effective bank oversight.

- The IMF should publish information on debt size and structure.

The Fund's brief should be to take a lead on these issues and to adjust the private sector's incentives. And this should be done soon.

Andrew Crockett
Bank for International Settlements

Andrew Crockett initially observed that the IMF is at the centre of the international monetary system, and will remain in this position. Reminding the audience of the observation by Padoa-Schioppa and Saccomani that the international monetary system is more market-based than government-based, Crockett noted that market-based systems are subject to failure. This is where improvements are most needed. The means should be better norms and standards, and more transparency. The Fund's tasks have become more complex in recent years. One reason is that financial markets have become more complex. Another reason is the gradual realization that structural issues deeply influence the macroeconomy and policy-making.

In responding to these challenges, should the IMF be seeking to expand its range of expertise? Crockett observed that the IMF is already spread very thin. He also cautioned against making the IMF too dominant an institution. One concern in this respect is that each rule has to be seen from different angles. Preserving some diversity of opinion and approach is the natural response.

Under these conditions, the best course for reform is to involve other types of expertise and to create committees to deal with important issues as they arise. A good recent example is the setting up of the Financial Stability Forum. This committee should now bring together the IMF, the World Bank and other institutions and define common procedures.

General Discussion

Richard Portes observed that the IMF currently plays too many roles. It is the investigator, the prosecutor, the prison warden, and the parole officer. A priority should be to narrow down its mandate.

Alexander Swoboda took up four main issues. On surveillance, he suggested that it should not only be carried out country by country but involve multilateral monitoring. On independence, he thought that political control is unavoidable: hence, the real question is how best to achieve political control. On pre-qualification to Fund programmes, he expressed support for the principle but foresaw severe political problems. Finally, he registered that US Treasury Secretary Rubin's statement discussed in the Report was so carefully stated that it was, in effect, empty.

Takatoshi Ito returned to the question of structural conditions. He recalled how, when the Thai crisis occurred during the summer of 1997, there was an obvious lack of coordination between the IMF and the World Bank. This coordination must be improved in the future. Second, to manage the Indonesian crisis in autumn 1997, the IMF treated the crisis as a balance of payments crisis, but it was mainly a political one. In Ito's view, the incorrect analysis of the Indonesian situation was very costly for this country. While the structural measures imposed by the IMF are certainly beneficial in the long run, they were simply impractical in that particular month.

More generally, Ito observed that structural problems exist elsewhere in the world. He asked why only Asian countries, where the problems are not the most acute, were singled out. For example, the Korean *chaebols* were not at the heart of the capital flow problem and did not require urgent dismantlement. Such a reform is better left for quiet periods, possibly under guidance by the World Bank. Regarding data dissemination, Ito noted that Thailand was in the SDSS at the time of its crisis and Brazil was not even a member of the GDDS. Yet, Thailand was not commended and Brazil was not punished.

Jon Cunliffe returned to the issue of surveillance. Noting that the IMF operates like a big orchestra with many players, he wondered how to avoid fragmentation of responsibility. This, he suggested, is where urgent reform is needed. It might mean that the Fund borrows experienced staff from supervisory and regulatory bodies. On independence, he observed that it is convenient to use the IMF as the tough guy who sends bad messages. As a consequence, its mandate is difficult to define and monitor. Cunliffe also stated that 'accountability to the Interim Committee' is a contradiction in terms. He feared that granting independence to the IMF would result in the dissipation of support for the institution.

Ian MacFarlane expressed concern about the tendency for a widening of structural policies in IMF programmes. He expressed support for drawing a clear line. For example, the IMF conditions should not have dealt with the car industry or the commercial shipbuilding industry in Indonesia.

Guillermo Perry further observed that while structural issues are critical for macroeconomic policies, they are not amenable to urgent action in the midst of a crisis. He supported the view that financial crisis resolution was a priority. Regarding the CCL, he wondered whether countries that are eligible would be interested in applying.

Shijuro Ogata suggested that reform of the IMF should include an enhanced role for the IMF in relation to the G-7 countries that no longer borrow from the IMF and thus do not listen to the IMF. Klaus Regling said that it is not possible to carry many reforms at the same time. He urged that a careful choice be made, and his priority list consists of discouraging short-term capital flows and *ex ante* crisis resolution. Luellen Stedman asked that the SDSS be given a chance to work. She also warned against the risk of caricature in describing the IMF as fulfilling too many roles. Andrew Crockett called for a clear definition of the structural issues that are thought to affect macroeconomic policies, and suggested that it was desirable to be limited and focused rather than to try to cover too much ground.

Endnotes

1. For example, the tax system might have to be overhauled and tax collectors trained. The banking system might have to be overhauled and licences given to promote competition and root out corruption. And going further, electricity might have to be provided to support these activities.
2. Evidence on such crisis triggers has been produced by Frankel and Rose (1996), Calvo et al. (1993) and Kaminsky and Reinhart (1999). .
3. The crises have been identified by Frankel and Rose (1986) as currency crashes, that is, sharp depreciations of the exchange rate in developing countries. The sample, which ends in 1992, is extended by the crises identified as successful speculative attacks by Kraay (1998), who looks at 75 middle- and high-income countries with populations greater than one million, over the period 1960–97. Kraay studies reserves losses.
4. Korea's exchange rate was allowed to fluctuate more freely in the years leading up to its crisis. But there is no question that investors believed that the authorities remained committed to preventing large fluctuations.
5. Note that, for historical reasons, Korea's quota is unusually small.
6. Number of votes = 250 + (quota/100 000).
7. We have first regressed country votes on the two characteristics to uncover the *de facto* statistical relationship that underpins the vote structure. We then use this relationship to compute each country's 'theoretical' voting share. Under- (over-) representation corresponds to the case where the actual share is lower (higher) than the computed 'theoretical' share.
8. If GNP alone is used as relevant variable, and trade is not considered, Belgium, the Netherlands and Switzerland are over-represented.
9. The Polak model was a path-breaking precursor of the Mundell-Fleming model and of the monetary approach to the balance of payments (both also developed at the Fund in the 1950s and 1960s), which are now standard fare in any textbook on open economy macroeconomics.
10. According to the press (*New York Times*, 16 February 1999), this position took form after a meeting of President Clinton with bankers

during his first campaign in 1992, which resulted in the Democratic Party's endorsement of a 'new economic world'.

11. The *Core Principles for Effective Banking Supervision* were recently issued by the Basle Committee on Banking Supervision and are intended to be 'a comprehensive blueprint for an effective supervisory system'. The committee itself was set up by the G-10 governors in 1974 with the aim of improving collaboration between bank supervisors in the light of the experiences earlier that year in connection with Bankhaus Herstatt in Germany and Franklin National Bank in New York.

12. The US Treasury seems to be considering a proposal that the IMF should recommend either flexible exchange rates or currency boards. IMF support will not be extended if a country adopts a fixed exchange rate regime (*Financial Times*, 22 April 1999). Excluding the middle ground between a currency board and a clean float generates several problems that need to be examined.

13. This is why the Argentine authorities have initiated discussions with the US Treasury on whether the United States would replace some of the country's forgone seigniorage out of the US budget.

14. The Financial Stability Forum was established by the G-7 in February 1999, at the suggestion of Bundesbank President Hans Tietmeyer. It is based in Basle under the umbrella of the BIS and is meant to coordinate international efforts at crisis prevention.

15. This section draws on Eichengreen and Rose (1999).

16. For example, IMF (1998), Kaminsky, Lizondo and Reinhart (1998), and Hardy and Pazarbasioglu (1998). For a detailed review of the evidence, see Berg and Pattillo (1998).

17. This is a variation of the Lucas critique. The application to early warning indicators was suggested by Ito (1998).

18. Recent work analyses the ability of markets to predict exchange rate movements. Goldfajn and Valdés (1998) use the *Financial Times* Forecaster Data to evaluate the ability of markets to predict crises using market expectations for exchange rates. They conclude that market expectations take into account real exchange rate misalignments, but fail to predict currency crises.

19. Could the IMF have issued a public warning expressing doubts about the exchange rate regime? Surely, doing so would have led to a much earlier collapse of the regime. In retrospect, it might have been a better outcome, but how could the IMF feel confident? Would not Thailand have felt that its sovereignty was violated?

20. A vocal exponent of this view is Martin Feldstein (Feldstein, 1998).

21. In 1998, in both Russia and Brazil, high-level IMF officials publicly professed full confidence that the agreed programmes were working and that there was no further currency risk, only to be proven wrong a few weeks later. Individual staff members, who were close to the

ground, privately recognized the mounting risks, but the IMF has a long tradition (well documented by Edwards, 1989) of enforcing hierarchical discipline.

22. SRFs were next used in Russia and Brazil, failing in both cases to achieve the stated aim of upholding a fixed exchange rate regime.

23. It is no secret that the United States had imposed pressures on the IMF to put together a large package for Mexico. The US bilateral part was collateralized by oil revenues separately from the IMF. And the IMF was angered that Mexico repaid the US portion of the package ahead of repaying the IMF portion.

24. Interestingly, 1997 is the year when the stand-by agreements were fewest. The table does not report other loans – extended and structural facilities – that have been introduced over the last decade. Even with these loans, the observations presented here would stand.

25. No G-7 countries other than Japan provided bilateral help as part of the Thailand package. The United States was asked to contribute bilaterally, but it declined. But the United States is said to have had an observer at the Tokyo meeting on 11 August, tracking what the IMF was doing in Bangkok.

26. Drazen and Masson (1994) draw an important distinction between credible policy-makers and credible policies. The former have a reputation for disciplined action while the latter are sustainable. Policy-makers who undertake policies that are meant to establish their dedication to disciplined action need to ascertain that the policies themselves are sustainable.

27. For a description of crises in Europe in 1992/3, see Eichengreen and Wyplosz (1993).

28. A systematic analysis by Borensztein and De Gregorio (1999) shows that the real depreciation is 70% of the initial nominal depreciation after three months, and 60% after two years.

29. For a detailed analysis of the structure of sharing, majority representation and collective representation clauses and their role in resolving crises, see Buchheit (1998a, b, c).

30. US and UK regulators, for their part, could make the admission of international bonds to their markets a function of whether those bonds contain the relevant sharing, majority voting, minimum legal threshold and collective representation provisions. They could include these same provisions in their own debt instruments.

31. This argument is formally established by Alesina and Drazen (1991). It is related to Mancur Olson's view that, as societies spontaneously get increasingly more complex and hard to change, extraordinary events like wars provide the only occasions when a clean-up is possible (see Olson, 1965).

32. Even if staff from different departments disagree with each other, management takes the decision before the Board meeting. Directors are not informed of disagreements among staff.

33. For details on composition of the Board, see www.imf.org/external/np/sec/memdir/eds.htm

34. Svensson (1999) advances analogous arguments for greater transparency of decision-making by national central banks. Faust and Svensson (1998) show how idiosyncratic goals affect incentives for transparency for national central banks, but their logic carries over to the IMF.

35. The Fund's experience with Russia is a case in point. After putting up an optimistic façade, the institution's reservations about the adequacy of the fiscal and financial reforms undertaken by Russian governments became increasingly evident over time.

36. Currently, Directors, Alternates and other representatives occupying Executive Board chairs are chosen by their constituencies. The governors of the IMF are usually finance ministers or heads of central banks, who propose and decide representation. Appointments last for two years and positions are rotated among countries. This rotation is up to the constituency.

37. Requiring a supermajority would protect Directors against the threat of arbitrary dismissal and therefore buttress their political independence.

References

Alesina, A. and A. Drazen (1991), 'Why Are Stabilizations Delayed?', *American Economic Review*, 81(5), 1170–88.

Berg, A. and C. Pattillo (1998), 'Are Currency Crises Predictable? A Test', IMF Working Paper No. WP/98/154.

Borensztein, E. and J. De Gregorio (1999), 'Devaluation and Inflation After Currency Crises', unpublished paper, Universidad de Chile, Santiago de Chile.

Buchheit, L. C. (1998a), 'Changing Bond Documentation: The Sharing Clause', International Financial Law Review (June), 17–19.

Buchheit, L. C. (1998b), 'Majority Action Clauses may Help Resolve Crises', *International Financial Law Review* (August), 9–10.

Buchheit, L. C. (1998c), 'The Collective Representation Clause', *International Financial Law Review* (September), 9–11.

Buiter, W. (1999), 'Alice in Euroland', *Journal of Common Market Studies* (June).

Calomiris, C. (1998), 'Blueprints for a New Global Financial Architecture', mimeo, Columbia University.

Calvo, G., L. Leiderman and C. Reinhart (1993), 'Capital Inflows and Real Exchange Rate Appreciation in Latin America: The Role of External Factors', IMF Staff Papers 40, pp.108–151.

Camdessus, M. (1995), 'Drawing Lessons from the Mexican Crisis: Preventing and Resolving Financial Crises - The Role of the IMF', address at the 25th Washington Conference of the Council of the Americas on 'Staying the Course: Forging a Free Trade Area in the Americas', Washington DC, 22 May.

CEPR (1998), *Financial Crises and Asia*, London.

Crockett, A. (1997), 'Why is Financial Stability a Goal of Public Policy?', in Federal Reserve Bank of Kansas City, *Maintaining Financial Stability in a Global Economy*, Kansas City.

Cuddington, J. (1989), 'The Extent and Causes of the Debt Crisis in the 1980s', in I. Husain and I. Diwan (eds), *Dealing with the Debt Crisis*, Washington DC: The World Bank, pp.15–42.

Cukierman, A. (1992), *Central Bank Strategy, Credibility and Independence*, Cambridge: MIT Press.

De Gregorio, J. and P. Guidotti (1995), 'Financial Development and Economic Growth', *World Development*, 23(3), 433–448.

De Gregorio, J., S. Edwards and R. Valdés (1999), 'Capital Controls in Chile: An Assessment', mimeo, Universidad de Chile.

Dornbusch, R. (1980), 'Exchange Rate Economics: Where Do We Stand?', *Brookings Papers on Economic Activity 1*, pp.143–85.

Dornbusch, R. (1998), 'After Asia: New Directions for the International Financial System', mimeo, MIT.

Drazen, A. and P. Masson (1994), 'Credibility of Policies versus Credibility of Policymakers', *Quarterly Journal of Economics*, 109(3), 735–54.

Edwards, S. (1989), 'The International Monetary Fund and the Developing Countries: A Critical Evaluation', *Carnegie-Rochester Conference Series on Public Policy 31*, pp.7–68.

Edwards, S. (1998a), 'Capital Flows, Real Exchange Rates, and Capital Controls: Some Latin American Experiences', NBER Working Paper No. 6800.

Edwards, S. (1998b), 'Abolish the IMF', *Financial Times* (13 November).

Eichengreen, B. (1999), *Toward a New International Financial Architecture: A Practical Post-Asia Agenda*, Washington DC: Institute for International Economics.

Eichengreen, B. and A. Mody (1998), 'Interest Rates in the North and Capital Flows to the South: Is There a Missing Link?', *International Finance*, 1, 35–58.

Eichengreen, B. and A. Rose (1999), 'Empirical Studies of Currency and Banking Crises', *NBER Reporter* (March).

Eichengreen, B., A. Rose and C. Wyplosz (1995), 'Exchange Rate Mayhem: The Antecedents and Aftermath of Speculative Attacks', *Economic Policy*, 21, 249–312.

Eichengreen, B. and C. Wyplosz (1993), 'The Unstable EMS', *Brookings Papers on Economic Activity 1*, 51–124.

Faust, J. and L. Svensson (1998), 'Transparency and Credibility: Monetary Policy with Unobservable Goals', NBER Working Paper No. 6452 (March).

Feldstein, M. (1998), 'Refocusing the IMF', *Foreign Affairs* (March/April), 20–33.

Feldstein, M. (1999), 'Self Help for Emerging Markets', *Foreign Affairs* (March/April).

Fischer, S., R. Sahay, and C. Vegh (1999), 'Modern High Inflation,' mimeo, IMF.

Fitch IBCA (1998), 'Asia: Agencies' Harsh Lessons in a Crisis', January.

Frankel, J. and A. Rose (1996), 'Currency Crashes in Emerging Markets', *Journal of International Economics*, 41(3-4), 351–66.

Frankel, J. and Schmukler (1996), 'Country Fund Discounts and the Mexican Crisis of December 1994: Did Local Residents Turn Pessimistic before International Investors?', *Open Economies Review*, 7(0), Supplement 1, 511–34.

Glick, R. and A. Rose (1998), 'Contagion and Trade: Why Are Currency Crises Regional?', CEPR Discussion Paper 1947.

Goldfajn, I. and R. Valdés (1998), 'Are Currency Crises Predictable?', *European Economic Review*, 42, 873–85.

Hardy, D. and C. Pazarbasioglu (1998), 'Leading Indicators of Banking Crises: Was Asia Different?', IMF Working Paper No. 98/91 (June).

IMF (1998), 'Financial Crises: Characteristics and Indicators of Vulnerability' in *World Economic Outlook*, chapter 4 (May).

Ito, T. (1998), 'Bail-out, Moral Hazard, and Credibility', paper presented at the Wharton Conference on Asian Twin Financial Crises, 10 March.

Ito, T., E. Ogawa and Y. N. Sasaki (1999), 'Establishment of the East Asian Fund', in *Stabilization of Currency and Financial Systems in East Asia and International Financial Coordination*, chapter 3, Tokyo: Institute for International Monetary Affairs.

Japan Center for International Finance (1999), *Characteristics and Appraisal of Major Rating Companies, 1999: Focusing on Ratings in Japan and Asia*, Tokyo.

Kaminsky, G. L., J. Lizondo and C. R. Reinhart (1998), 'Leading Indicators of Currency Crises', *IMF Staff Papers*, 45(1), March, 1–48.

Kaminsky, G. L. and C. R. Reinhart (1999), 'The Twin Crises: The Causes of banking and Balance-of-Payments problems', *American Economic Review*, 89(3), 473–500.

Kraay, A. (1998), 'Do High Interest Rates Defend Currencies During Speculative Attacks?', unpublished paper, The World Bank.

Lane, T., A. R. Ghosh, J. Hamann, S. Phillips, M. Schulze-Ghattas and T. Tsikata (1999), 'IMF-Supported Programmes in Indonesia, Korean and Thailand: A Preliminary Assessment', mimeo, IMF, www.imf.org/.

Lerrick, A. (1999), 'Private Sector Financing for the IMF: Now Part of an Optimal Funding Mix', Bretton Woods Committee, Washington DC.

Lora, E. (1997), 'A Decade of Structural Reforms in Latin America: What Has Been Reformed and How to Measure It', IBD Working Paper Green Series No. 348.

Miyazawa, K. (1999), 'Statement at the World Bank Symposium on Global Finance and Development', Tokyo, 1 March.

Nadal de Simone, F. and P. Sorsa (1999), 'Capital Account Restrictions in Chile in the 1990s', mimeo, IMF.

Nordhaus, W. (1975), 'The Political Business Cycle', *Review of Economic Studies*, 42,169–190.

Olson, M. (1965), *The Logic of Collective Action*, Cambridge: Harvard University Press.

Polak, J. J. (1957), 'Monetary Analysis of Income Formation and Payments Problems', IMF Staff Papers 6, pp.1–50.

Polak, J. J. (1997), 'The IMF Monetary Model at Forty', IMF Working Paper WP/97/49 (April).

Posen, A. (1995), 'Declarations are Not Enough: Financial Sector Sources of Central Bank Independence', *NBER Macroeconomics Annual*, Cambridge: MIT Press, pp.349–55.

Radelet, S. and J. Sachs (1998), 'The East Asian Financial Crisis: Diagnosis, Remedies, Prospects', *Brookings Papers on Economic Activity 1*, pp. 1–90.

Rodrik, D. (1998), Who Needs Capital-Account Convertibility?', *Essays in International Finance No. 207*, Princeton University, pp.55–65.

Rogoff, K. (1985), 'The Optimal Degree of Commitment to an Intermediate Monetary Target', *Quarterly Journal of Economics*, 100, pp.1169–89.

Rojas-Suárez, L. and S. Weisbrod (1996), 'Banking Crises in Latin America: Experiences and Issues', in R. Hausmann and L. Rojas-Suárez (eds), *Banking Crises in Latin America*, Washington DC: Inter-American Development Bank/Johns Hopkins University Press.

Sachs, J. (1998), 'Proposals for Reform of the Global Financial Architecture', unpublished manuscript, Harvard University.

Sargent, T. and N. Wallace (1981), 'Some Unpleasant Monetary Arithmetic', *Federal Reserve Bank of Minneapolis Quarterly Review*, 5, 1–17.

Stiglitz, J. E. (1999), 'On Liberty, the Right to Know, and Public Discourse: The Role of Transparency in Public Life', Oxford, Amnesty Lecture, 27 January.

Svensson, L. (1999), 'Monetary Policy Issues for the ECB', *Carnegie-Rochester Conference Series on Public Policy*.

van Wincoop (1994), 'Welfare Gains from International Risk Diversification', *Journal of Monetary Economics*, 34, 175–200.

World Bank (1997), *Private Capital Flows to Developing Countries*, Oxford: Oxford University Press.

Wyplosz, C. (1998), 'Speculative Attacks and Capital Mobility', mimeo, Graduate Institute of International Studies, Geneva.